Part 2
Digging Deeper

**Moving from
Shattered to Strong**

THE FOUNDATIONS OF RECOVERY

From Sexual Addiction And Intimacy Avoidance

**Matt Burton
Kevin Rose
Laura Burton**

Part 2
Digging Deeper

Moving from Shattered to Strong

THE FOUNDATIONS OF RECOVERY

From Sexual Addiction And Intimacy Avoidance

MATT BURTON
KEVIN ROSE
LAURA BURTON

Part 2
Digging Deeper

Moving from
Shattered to Strong

THE
FOUNDATIONS
OF RECOVERY

From Sexual Addiction
And Intimacy Avoidance

MATT BURTON
KEVIN ROSE
LAURA BURTON

Copyright © 2025 by Becoming Well, LLC

All rights reserved. No part of this book may be reproduced or transmitted in any form, or by any means, electronic or mechanical, including photocopying, recording, or by information storage or retrieval systems, without permission in writing from the copyright owner.

The views and opinions expressed in this book are those of the author and do not necessarily reflect the official policy or position of Becoming Well, LLC

Published by Becoming Well, LLC

www.BecomingWellInstitute.com

Library of Congress Control Number

Paperback ISBN: 979-8-3493-8685-5

E-book ISBN: 979-8-3493-8686-2

Cover design by Monira

Printed in the United States of America

Table of Contents

Are You All In? 3
1. Exercise Book Completed in a Year 4
2. 3 Goals 5
3. 5 Stages of Change 7
4. Spiritual Bypassing 8
5. Wrong Thinking 10
6. Lust vs Recovery Based Decision 13
7. 1st, 2nd, 3rd, and 4th Gear 15
8. Owning It Letter 17

Lying 21
9. Lying 22
10. Outright Lying 23
11. Omitting the Truth 25
12. Gaslighting 27
13. Character Lying 29
14. Dribble Disclosure 31

Objectification 33
15. Battle Against Objectification 34
16. Pray to Humanize 35
17. Do the Opposite 37
18. Flush the Toilet 39
19. Caught Looking – Real or Perceived 41
20. Look Up 43
21. Positioning 45
22. Eye Contact 47
23. One Second 49
24. Don't Use Your Partner to Masturbate 51

Helping Your Partner Heal (Part 2) — 53
- 25. Wounding Agent vs Healing Agent — 54
- 26. Coercive Sex - Cup of Tea — 55
- 27. Drama Triangle — 57
- 28. Time Out Protocol — 59
- 29. Demeanor Part 2 — 61
- 30. The Cynical Script — 63
- 31. Apology Language — 65
- 32. Reparations — 67
- 33. Love Language Sandwich — 69
- 34. Importance of Dates — 71

Warning Signs — 73
- 35. SA/PA Warning Signs — 75
- 36. Price of Addiction — 77
- 37. Tips to Avoid Relapse — 79
- 38. IA Warning Signs — 81
- 39. How to Spot IA Behaviors — 83
- 40. Middle of the Roof — 85
- 41. Anger and Resentment Letter — 87
- 42. Releasing Anger and Resentment — 93
- 43. Affair Types — 96
- 44. Cascade Towards Betrayal — 98

Marathon of Recovery — 99
- 45. Self-Care Plan — 101
- 46. Self-Care Schedule — 103
- 47. Flawed and Loved — 105
- 48. Daily 10th Step Inventory — 107
- 49. The Hot Seat — 109
- 50. Recovery Travel Plan — 111
- 51. Life in Recovery — 115
- 52. Sponsoring Others — 117

Addendum — 121
40 ways to be IA (Intimacy Avoidant) — 129
Workgroups and Intensives — 135
Books and Courses — 143

AUTHORS' NOTE

Although the publisher and the authors have made every effort to ensure that the information in this book was correct at press time, and while this publication is designed to provide accurate information regarding the subject matter covered, the publisher and the authors assume no responsibility for errors, inaccuracies, omissions, or any other inconsistencies herein and hereby disclaim any liability to any party for any loss, damage, or disruption caused by errors or omissions, whether such errors or omissions result from negligence, accident, or any other cause.

This publication is meant as a source of valuable information for the reader. However, it is not meant as a substitute for direct expert assistance. If such a level of assistance is required, the services of a competent professional should be sought.

MATT AND LAURA BURTON
www.BecomingWellInstitute.com

INTRODUCTION

Welcome to Foundations of Recovery. Regardless of where you're at on your recovery journey, this workbook will help you chart a path of health. It will also benefit those hurt by your destructive behaviors and the ways of thinking connected to them. In short, *Foundations of Recovery* will help you get better.

This workbook was birthed out of 30-plus years of personal recovery and walking with thousands of men through their recovery journeys. Whether you are working on *Foundations of Recovery – Part 1: Ground Zero*, or *Foundations of Recovery – Part 2: Digging Deeper*, you will find that the exercises in this workbook will expand the depth of your recovery. It will also provide you with many, many tools to help you navigate and succeed in your individual and relational recovery.

Foundations of Recovery – Part 1: Ground Zero focuses on expanding your recovery toolbox, getting through the 12 steps in a year, and doing exercises around helping your partner heal, as well as maintaining a sobriety focus.

Foundations of Recovery – Part 2: Digging Deeper focuses on whether you are "all in" with regards to recovery, how to understand the destructiveness of lying and exercises to combat it, how objectification is so destructive, and how to change object thinking. It also offers a focus on helping your partner heal. You will be educated on the warning signs of potential relapse and given the tools you need to journey long-term through the marathon that is recovery.

Each workbook contains 52 exercises. We hope you will complete at least one exercise per week and finish this workbook in one year. For those wishing to accelerate their recovery, you will complete two exercises per week: one in *Foundations of Recovery – Part 1: Ground Zero*, and one in *Foundations of Recovery – Part 2: Digging Deeper*. Do this and you'll complete both workbooks in a year. Whether you get them done in one or two years, these workbooks, when done weekly and shared with your partner, will help you profoundly in your individual and relational recovery journey.

Other materials available through Becoming Well, LLC and our Becoming Well Institute here in Tucson, AZ, may be helpful in your journey. They are listed in the appendix of this book with a full list on our website. Virtual sessions for individuals and couples, Recovery Workgroups, Couples Private Intensives, Couples Group Intensives, Wounded Partner Healing Intensives, Men's Recovery Intensives, and Men's Going Deeper Healing Intensives, as well as courses, books, and videos are also available worldwide.

Please contact us for further information. You can visit our website at www.BecomingWellInstitute.com for access other resources for you and your partner

Becoming Well, LLC and Becoming Well Institute
phone number: 520-355-5322
Email address: Info@MyBecomingWell.com

Are You All In?

THE FOUNDATIONS OF RECOVERY - PART 2 DIGGING DEEPER

 Exercise 1

Exercise Book Completed in a Year

Between the two exercise books offered by The Becoming Well Institute, you will have 100 total exercises in each workbook to complete over the course of one year. Doing the math, this means 2 exercises per week. Pairing this expectation with the **Daily Times for Recovery**, you will be on track to complete them all. *Be aware that if you're in a Becoming Well Workgroup, you will have planned exercises (homework) to complete and discuss while in group 2-3 times monthly. This counts towards your expectation of 2 exercises per week.

Why do you have this expectation for yourself? Part of your growth in recovery, whether you are in a relationship or not, is creating habits of daily recovery for the rest of your life. Like your physical body, your heart and spirit need exercise to remain healthy. If you don't stay in recovery, you will drift out of health.

Think of a healthy habit you have developed in your life. How has it benefited you?

If you haven't kept up with the habit listed above, what did you begin to lose?

If you are ready to commit to this practice, this is great news! Share it with a recovery partner in a workgroup and a sponsor. *I, _____(name), say _____(yes/no), I will commit to completing two exercises per week during my Daily Times for Recovery.*

Steps 1-3 Connection: When we come together to recover, we do so with the power of accountability.

Share your commitment with another person.

How does it feel to be in community with others who are also seeking health?

On a recovery call, ask someone what this commitment has produced for them. Record their answer here.

PARTNER CONNECT Share your commitment to completing the 52 exercises with your partner. Who are you going to choose as an accountability partner to help hold you to this commitment?

ARE YOU ALL IN?

3 Goals

Exercise 2

If you don't have a goal, you're not going to reach it. In individual recovery and relational recovery, it's vital to make sure that you have goals that you both write out and periodically check to make sure that you are executing them well.

That's where 3 & 3 come in:
- 3 individual recovery goals
- 3 relationship recovery goals.

These are 12-month goals. Next, you're going to write out three individual recovery goals.

Make these for yourself, for your SA recovery, and for your IA recovery.

1.

2.

3.

Next, you're going to write out relationship goals. Again, do these independent of your partner. Make it come from your heart and your desires for your partnership.

1.

2.

3.

Share your relational goals with your partner. In these beginning stages of recovery, whatever their feelings may be about your goals, practice the **Empathy Exercise** regarding their feelings. Reflect here on your partner's feelings and how they are understandable in this stage of recovery.

Feeling_____ Why it's understandable:

Feeling_____ Why it's understandable:

Step 1 Connection: The powerlessness of this step is also designed to have you reflect on what is in your power. In a calendar one year from now, whether digitally in your device or on a hardcopy calendar, set a reminder to reflect on your 3 & 3.

THE FOUNDATIONS OF RECOVERY - PART 2 DIGGING DEEPER

PARTNER CONNECT Share your goals with your partner.

5 Stages of Change   Exercise 3

There are 5 stages of making a change:

1. **Precontemplation**   Not yet acknowledging there is a problem that needs to change
   This is a stage where you are resistant and in denial of the seriousness of your need for recovery. Pride is at the heart of this stage.

2. **Contemplation**   Acknowledging and wanting to make a change
   This is a place of being on the fence about recovery. You may be wrestling with guilt and want change, but you may be stuck here if your actions aren't lining up with what you say you want.

3. **Preparation**   Being ready to make changes
   You have committed to change! This is accompanied by the question, "What can I do?" The heart here is humble and wanting to seek any means to the end of the destruction of SA or IA.

4. **Action**   Changing behaviors and using any tool necessary to do so
   You feel motivated here! This stage can often come and go in waves, since our willpower is not what will get us through ongoing lifelong recovery. See Step 3.

5. **Maintenance**   Frequently reflecting and revising/adding plans for ongoing change
   Reflect, Revise, and Anticipate. Once you are in maintenance, there is a responsibility to either continue to see the need for recovery or not.

Now, it is normal to go between some or all 5 of the stages in a day. Over the course of the next week, identify the stages you are in each day and describe how you could tell you were in that stage.

Day	Stages	Describe Why You Were in That Stage
1		
2		
3		
4		
5		
6		
7		

Step 1 Connection: Why are you powerless over what you are recovering from?

PARTNER CONNECT Share the information you have learned about the 5 Stages of Change with your partner.

 **Exercise 4**   **Spiritual Bypassing**

What Is Spiritual Bypassing?

Spiritual bypassing describes a tendency to use spiritual explanations to avoid complex psychological issues.

Spiritual bypassing can be defined as:

"a tendency to use spiritual ideas and practices to sidestep or avoid facing unresolved emotional issues, psychological wounds, and unfinished developmental tasks."

Spiritual bypassing is a superficial way of glossing over problems that might make us feel better in the short term, but ultimately solves nothing and just leaves the problem to linger on.

Spiritual bypassing is also often used to dismiss the very real concerns of people who are dealing with problems.

Before resorting to platitudes, ask yourself who the comment is really helping. Are you really giving someone comfort or insight, or is it just a way of dismissing a difficult situation so that you can feel better?

Causes

Spiritual bypassing acts as a form of defense mechanism. It protects us from things that seem too painful to deal with, but this protection comes at a cost. Ignoring or avoiding the issue can make stress worse in the long-term and make the problem more difficult to solve later on. While avoidance is a primary motivator behind this type of behavior, there are other factors that play a role in shaping it.

Impacts

Spiritual bypassing isn't always a bad thing. In times of severe distress, it can be a way to temporarily relieve frustration or anxiety. However, researchers suggest that it can be damaging when used as a long-term strategy to suppress problems.

Spiritual bypassing can have a few negative effects. It can affect individual well-being as well as relationships with others. Some of the potential negative consequences include:

- Anxiety
- Blind allegiance to leaders
- Codependency
- Control problems
- Disregard for personal responsibility
- Emotional confusion
- Excessive tolerance of unacceptable or inappropriate behavior
- Feelings of shame

Spiritual narcissism

Spiritual narcissism involves using spiritual practices to increase self-importance. It often involves using spirituality to build the individual up, while also wielding it as a weapon to tear others down.

Step 4 Connection: Complete an entry for your inventory

Subject	What Happened	My Reaction (Door A)	My Reason
Spiritual Bypassing *List the people, places, or groups*	*Tell the story(ies) of when you withdraw with* <u>***Spiritual Bypassing***</u>	*Describe your feelings and behaviors*	*Name the nature of your reasons (ex: fear, selfishness, prideful, control, comfort...)*

THE FOUNDATIONS OF RECOVERY - PART 2 DIGGING DEEPER

Exercise 5 — Wrong Thinking

Unless you become aware of false ways of thinking, you'll forever be at risk of falling back into the same traps. Changing belief systems takes diligence, but it is possible. The first step is learning to identify the **lies we believe**. The second is **replacing your wrong thinking with truth**.

- **Seeking sympathy** – you do and say things to get others to feel sorry for you
- **Victim thinking** – this allows you to avoid taking personal responsibility through powerlessness
- **Instant gratification** – this is a thinking pattern that causes you to be self-centered and to want things now. It is characterized by impatience and selfishness.
- **Blame** – this is another way of avoiding personal responsibility. It allows you to justify your behavior based on what others do.
- **Everybody's Doing It** – This pattern of thinking allows people to justify abandoning their personal commitments, morals, and beliefs because others are doing the same thing.
- **Uniqueness** – With this thinking error, you believe that the rules don't apply to you. This allows you to make yourself different from others.
- **Anger** – This thinking pattern is used to control and manipulate others. If you are confronted about a behavior that is inappropriate, outrage and anger can cause all the attention to be directed at the anger, rather than at the criticism of your behaviors or attitudes.
- **My Way** – This thinking reveals a strong desire for power. Someone using this thinking pattern resists being under the control or power of someone else. They want things to be done on their terms and under their conditions.
- **The "Good One"** – With this thinking error, your present yourself as sentimental and think of yourself as mostly good, and not someone who is in need of grace. In fact, you may even believe that your higher power is fortunate to have you as their child because of all the good you're going to do in their world. This image of yourself as good is maintained through the good words you perceive yourself doing. This "good guy" image is, however, quickly abandoned in search for the gratification of your addiction and for excitement in general. You use sentimentality and your good works as a way to build up your opinion of yourself as a good person. Addicts will readily sacrifice others in their pursuit of sexual and other devious goals.
- **Hop-over** – this is a way of shifting a conversation to something more comfortable. By hopping over the real question, we control others, especially if they answer the question.
- **Reckless Attitude** – This pattern of thinking causes you to avoid behaviors that are seen as difficult, boring, distasteful, hard, or disagreeable. This way of thinking causes you to avoid activities where change is slow and rewards for change seem too small. Motivation and energy for responsible living is low, but energy and motivation for risky, illegal, or forbidden acts is high.
- **Minimizing** – this is a common tendency where you believe that what you have done is really not that important. By taking one aspect of reality and minimizing it, you're able to minimize the entire act in your mind. When we minimize our actions, they seem to become unimportant, insignificant, and not really that bad. We attempt to make something big into something small.

ARE YOU ALL IN?

In the table below, identify (with your partner if they're open to it) which patterns of thinking you will slip into. You will eventually slip back into wrong thinking. Your mind has been prone to think wrongly for so long. List what you think you are gaining in the **wrong thinking**. Then, list what you will gain if you change your thoughts into **correct thinking.**

Wrong Thinking	What You Think You Gain	Correct Thinking and What You'll Gain

THE FOUNDATIONS OF RECOVERY - PART 2 DIGGING DEEPER

Step 10 Connection: Part of your ongoing inventory, which you have completed above, is to confess it to another person in recovery. Make a call this week. Tell someone about the wrong thinking you are recovering from. Ask them if they have been in your shoes with any of the same wrong thoughts. Then for the similarities, ask and record below what they do to correct their **wrong thinking.**

PARTNER CONNECT Using your best self-reflection skills, share what you have learned about yourself through this exercise with your partner.

ARE YOU ALL IN?

Lust vs Recovery Based Decision

Exercise 6

Each day we are faced with many different types of decisions. When seeking to obtain a lust hit or fix for our sexual drives, we leave breadcrumbs of many smaller decisions that lead up to those decisions. This exercise is meant to trace and uncover the crumbs you leave behind whenever you seek a lust hit. You can use the *3 Circles* exercise along with many of the other exercises in the Getting Started and Rigorous Honesty sections to help.

It comes down to identifying boundaries for yourself. Set guardrails so you can stay on the narrow path of recovery.

What do you watch? Reflect here on what types of media and entertainment you let into your eyes.

Identify boundaries you need to put in place to stay out of lustful thinking.

(Examples: TV Shows, Movies, Apps on your phone…)

Who do you spend time with? This is a tough one. Identify people you spend your time with that do and don't support your walk away from sexual addiction. Whether you've told them or not, they have an influence on your life. Reflect on who is safe for you to spend time with.

Where do you go? Reflect on your commute and places you visit/vacation to. Create boundaries for where you go. This could be as simple as taking a different route to get to work.

THE FOUNDATIONS OF RECOVERY - PART 2 DIGGING DEEPER

Step 5 Connection: To another person in recovery, admit the decisions you plan to make to stay in recovery. Ask them and record here what decisions they have made.

[ ]

PARTNER CONNECT Once you have admitted to someone in recovery your decisions regarding what you will and won't do to stay in recovery, share the same information with your partner.

ARE YOU ALL IN?

1st, 2nd, 3rd, and 4th Gear

Exercise 7

Consider a manual drive vehicle. You start in neutral and shift up one gear at a time.

Let's break down your Recovery as Gears from 1-4.

1st Gear: Work on Your Recovery
SA – This involves going to meetings, staying sober, setting up boundaries whenever needed, and any other recovery tool in this book or found elsewhere that you use
IA – For intimacy growth, 80% of your work is relational between you and your partner while 20% is completing book work, doing exercises, and making recovery calls

2nd Gear: Create Safety for Your Partner
Whatever SA/Infidelity or IA recovery stage you are in, create safety with consistency over long periods of time. This is what we call your sobriety date. Until your partner feels safe, practice letting go your needs and selflessly giving what your partner needs.

Now your partner begins engaging in recovery themselves.

3rd Gear: Wounded Partners begin daily/weekly self-evaluation
Supporting your partner in this gear means opening up conversation with compassion for where they are in recovery. It is important to also keep your momentum from the 1st and 2nd gears.
*Playing the victim about how your partner is NOT in recovery themselves will never help the relationship feel safe enough for your partner. Remember that the betrayal has left them wondering if you will ever be trustworthy again, and you are responsible for the devastation caused by your behavior(s).

4th Gear: With both partners active in pursuing one another, this is what makes for a great relationship!

Which gear are you currently in? Why?

With your partner, discuss what the gear the relationship is in. Revisit what actions you can take on a day-to-day basis to help your partner feel safe in the relationship.

THE FOUNDATIONS OF RECOVERY - PART 2 DIGGING DEEPER

Step 7 Connection: Humbly going to your higher power and praying for aid is a practice, not perfection. Write a prayer using the P-R-A-Y template below.

P – Praise Thank your higher power for…	
R – Reveal Confess, open a heart to repent for…	
A – Ask Petition the higher power for aid in…	
Y – Yield Give control over to your higher power for your life and will (Step 3)	

PARTNER CONNECT Be sure to discuss Part 2 of this exercise with your partner.

Owning It Letter

Exercise 8

Think about your partner's apology language. Refer to the previous exercise. Taking full responsibility with a letter is merely words on a page. What is going to matter the most when you read this letter to your partner is your demeanor. Below is an example of how you can write the introduction and body of your letter.

Introduction

> To _____ (my partner),

> You have devoted _____ years, _____ decades (if applicable) of your life to me.

> *You trusted me with your heart, to care for you emotionally, to have compassion and empathy for you. You trusted me to be faithful to you. You trusted me to make you my greatest priority, day in and day out. You trusted me to give all of me to you. You trusted me to love you, hear you, value you, care for you, protect you, validate you. I made a vow to do all these things and I didn't.*

Body (sentence frames & examples)

I promised/committed to_____, and I didn't.

> *I promised I'd see the best in you, and I didn't. I saw whatever I felt like I needed to, to justify my wrong actions.*

> *I promised to hear you, to value your insight, opinions, and thoughts, and I didn't. Instead, I shifted the blame to shine the light away from my selfishness.*

> *I promised to praise you, to build you up and share everything with you and the world because you are great, and I didn't.*

> *I promised I'd love you, not in the way that suited me but in the ways that you experience love, and I didn't.*

I take full responsibility for_____. That's on me, that's not on you.

> *I'm 100% responsible for the devastation I've caused and 100% responsible for my recovery from it.* **That's not on you, that's on me. You have no responsibility in that.**

> *I've played the victim in nearly every area of our relationship, rather than growing up and taking responsibility for what I've done. That's not on you, that's on me. You have no responsibility in that.*

I've been_____, doing _____ to you, treating you _____. That's on me, that's not on you.

> *I've been selfish, at some point making anything and everything about me. That's not on you, that's on me. You have no responsibility in that.*

You haven't been treated with the love, respect, or care that you should have. That's not on you, that's on me. You have no responsibility in that.

I showed you over and over that what I protected was myself, not you. Of course you don't feel loved by me. My actions and attitudes towards you haven't shown that. That's not on you, that's on me. You have no responsibility in that.

Your Owning It Letter

___

ARE YOU ALL IN?

THE FOUNDATIONS OF RECOVERY - PART 2 DIGGING DEEPER

Step 9 Connection: You will write a section in your amends letter that is like this Owning It letter. When you are prepared, be open to asking if your partner will forgive you. Still, it is important to be open to their "no" as an answer. This is because, in their healing process from pain, they might not be ready to forgive yet. That is ok and understandable. Write how you would feel if they were ready to forgive and said "yes I forgive you," or if they said "no I don't/can't forgive you yet."

"yes"

"no"

Lying

 **Exercise 9** — **Lying**

Most wounded partners tell us that, as hard as it is to forgive betrayal, it's even harder to forgive the deception surrounding the betrayal. The fact that the wounding partner had a secret life that they knew nothing about can be a hard thing to get over. It is even harder to get over when someone keeps lying. After a while, the wounded partner begins to wonder if the wounding partner is even capable of telling the truth. This can seriously affect their willingness to move forward with the relationship.

Additionally, when the wounding partner repeatedly lies, they send the message that they are more interested in protecting themselves than they are in caring for their partner's broken heart.

Trust is pivotal to all healthy relationships. The whole reason we do the work we do is to help couples rebuild the trust that has been torn down by betrayal. Lying and deception not only break trust, but they also lead to more lies and deception to cover up the initial lying and deception. This results in a never-ending downward spiral that ultimately leads to the complete breakdown of the relationship.

Lying also prevents the deep, important conversations that are at the core of committed relationships from happening because distrust can often lead to withdrawal on the wounded partner's part. A lack of communication will also lead to a breakdown of the relationship.

Outright lying, half-truths, lies by omission, character lies, and even carelessness with seemingly minor details will hamper momentum toward the recovery of the relationship. The next few exercises are dedicated to these different categories of lies.

How does lying break down and harm a relationship?

Why is lying to someone against your moral code? Explain a time when you were guilty of lying.

Step 4 Connection: At the heart of your lies, what did you think you were gaining when you lied to your partner?

PARTNER CONNECT If you have been lying to your partner, you must admit this to them. Make a recovery phone call to prepare yourself. At a calm moment, admit to your partner what you have been lying to them about. Make a recovery phone call after you have the discussion to process what was said.

LYING

Outright Lying

Exercise 10

Refer to the *Lying* exercise for definitions and explanations around the consequences of lying.

Here in this exercise, you will recall times in which you have outright lied in order to avoid intimacy or hide your sexual addiction. If you keep any of these lies hidden, betrayal is multiplied by the duration you have kept the lie to yourself. The table below is broken into the Situations you've lied about, the IA or SA Behavior behind the lie, and the Consequences of keeping each lie hidden. *Use additional paper if needed.

Outright Lie Situation	IA or SA Behavior	Consequences

THE FOUNDATIONS OF RECOVERY - PART 2 DIGGING DEEPER

Step 4 Connection: Count these entries towards your inventory. In general, know how lying has benefited you throughout your life and in general how has lying damaged your relationships.

PARTNER CONNECT With your partner, discuss what you have learned about your tendency to lie. Share with them why you think you do it. If there are things you have lied to them about, admit it to them. Make a recovery phone call to make sure you are in the right frame of mind to do this without defending or getting angry. Make a recovery phone call after you talk to your partner to help you process what was said.

Omitting the Truth

Exercise 11

Refer to the *Lying* exercise for definitions and explanations around the consequences of lying.

Here in this exercise, you will recall times in which you have lied by omission in order to avoid intimacy or hide your sexual addiction. If you keep any of these lies hidden, betrayal is multiplied by the duration you have kept the lie to yourself. The table below is broken into the Situations you've lied about, the IA or SA Behavior behind the lie, and the Consequences of keeping each lie hidden. *Use additional paper if needed.

Omission Situation	IA or SA Behavior Most Related	Relational Consequences

THE FOUNDATIONS OF RECOVERY - PART 2 DIGGING DEEPER

Step 5 Connection: On a recovery call this week, confess these situations you have lied. Make sure to explain what the consequences are. Record the feelings you felt confessing and why.

PARTNER CONNECT If you have lied by omission to your partner, you will need to admit this to them. Prepare yourself to do this by making a recovery phone call and/or discussing it during group. Once you have prepared, tell your partner how you have lied by omission. Make a recovery phone call after you talk to your partner to help you process what was discussed.

Gaslighting

Exercise 12

This is the action of deliberately wounding a partner by:

- Questioning their reality or what they are experiencing
- Creating a prison of psychological trauma, anxiety, isolation, and depression
- Refusing to admit past gaslighting actions (a continual gaslighting)

Here are the different modes of gaslighting found in dysfunctional relationships:

- **Countering:** Questioning someone's memory of events
- **Withholding**: Pretending not to understand what someone is talking about or refusing to accept the validity of someone's experience
- **Forgetting**: Pretending to have forgotten something or denying that something happened
- **Trivializing**: Making someone's concerns or feelings seem unimportant or irrational
- **Diverting/Blocking:** Changing the subject or focusing on the credibility of what is being said instead of the content. (This can be a focus on specific facts rather than the general issue)

If you've gaslighted in your relationship, the good news is you can take responsibility today. But what does it sound like when you gaslight? Here are some examples:

"You never remember things correctly."
"I never said that."
"You're being too sensitive."
"That never happened."
"I never understand what you're talking about."
"Your memory is bad. You need to see someone."
"You seem off. You need help."
"You're crazy."
"The kids think you're crazy."
"This is why you don't have any friends."
"You can never take a joke."
"You're the one gaslighting me."

I gaslight by saying…

What are the motives behind why you gaslight?

Discuss this with another in recovery who also has this struggle.

Step 6 Connection: Ask your higher power for the removal of this defect of character. Acknowledge the pain it has caused. Praise your higher power and choose to trust that they can help you eliminate thoughts and words that would hurt your partner.

THE FOUNDATIONS OF RECOVERY - PART 2 DIGGING DEEPER

PARTNER CONNECT Gaslighting has hurt your partner. It has messed with their sense of reality and has made them feel crazy. If you have been gaslighting your partner, or have gaslighted them in the past, you must admit it to them. Make a recovery phone call to get your head in the right space to admit ways in which you have gaslighted your partner. In a calm moment, tell them. Make a recovery phone call after the conversation to help you process what was discussed.

Character Lying

Exercise 13

Refer to the *Lying* exercise for definitions and explanations around the consequences of lying.

Here in this exercise, you will recall times in which you have lied to protect your ego, avoid intimacy, or hide your sexual addiction. If you keep any of these lies hidden, betrayal is multiplied by the duration you have kept the lie to yourself. The table below is broken into the Situations you've lied about, the IA or SA Behavior behind the lie, and the Consequences of keeping each lie hidden. *Use additional paper if needed.

Omission Situation	IA or SA Behavior Most Related	Relational Consequences

THE FOUNDATIONS OF RECOVERY - PART 2 DIGGING DEEPER

Step 6 Connection: Pride is at the heart of a character lie. Write a prayer expressing an open heart to transformation. Sit with the humility of the pain your pride has caused. Then humbly ask your higher power to help remove the pride that has driven you to inflate your ego.

PARTNER CONNECT Using your best self-reflection skills, share what you have learned about yourself with your partner.

LYING

Dribble Disclosure

Exercise 14

This terminology, dribble disclosure, is used to describe truth that is revealed slowly over time. What motivates someone who has wronged their partner is fear. Fear has driven you towards hiding the truth because you think that you are protecting the relationship.

Is this true about your story? Have you withheld the full truth in fear of losing your partner, or with a misconception of not wanting to cause them pain? Answer these questions and express your motivations to withhold the full truth.

[ ]

Research has shown that the deception over a long period of time is harder to get over than the infidelity itself. This is because the path towards rebuilding trust is marked with honesty. When that honesty is tarnished over time by continued deception, rebuilding trust is exponentially more difficult.

Through the view of your partner, why would it be difficult for them to trust you if you dribbled your disclosure?

[ ]

The hope you can have is that, once you have been fully honest, then and only then can you look forward to your partner, in time, participating in building a loving relationship through trust and commitment. Before that day of full honesty and transparency, your partner will wonder if the truth is all there. A polygraph can be helpful here to a) show your partner your willingness to prove, to the highest measure, your full honesty and disclosure of infidelity and b) provide enough safety for your partner to consider engaging in building trust in the relationship.

Step 7 Connection: By humbly asking your higher power to remove your character defect of lying, you are opening yourself up to the possibility of living a more full and intimate life. Describe the feeling you and your partner would have if rigorous honesty became a norm in the relationship, and if both of you felt safe to do so.

[ ]

Objectification

THE FOUNDATIONS OF RECOVERY - PART 2 DIGGING DEEPER

 **Exercise 15**   **Battle Against Objectification**

This is an exercise specific to the problem of lust and the objectification of anything or anyone that is the subject of our sexual addiction. This is the battle of the heart. Many times, addicts will express that they can't help thinking sexual thoughts. This is due in part to a psychological freeway of pleasure associated with modes of "acting out" such as fantasy and pornography. To turn off the freeway, we must pave a new road, humanizing the person of our lustful temptation.

Objectification can happen at any given moment. While driving, watching TV, at work, or even towards our partner, we diminish someone to a body part to be used in our sexual addiction. Yes, looking at our partners, lovers, or spouses as an object of sexual pleasure leaves no room for treating them as humans.

Name the places/areas in which objectification occurs.

[ ]

Next, we battle objectification by humanizing the people. List the human character traits or identities of the people you objectify. (Ex: mother, daughter, _____(career), sister, child of God, _____ (personality trait)…)

[ ]

Write a prayer for the most recent person you objectified, highlighting their human identity. Refer to the exercise *pray to humanize* for assistance.

[ ]

Step 4 Connection: Make a list of times (in general) when you objectified for your sexual addiction. Add these general mistreatments to your inventory of sexual addiction.

[ ]

PARTNER CONNECT This exercise should not be shared with your partner, as the information here will likely cause them pain.

OBJECTIFICATION

Pray to Humanize

Exercise 16

When our mind wanders, whether into lust, fantasy, or *negative narrative*, we can choose in that moment to snap our *rubber band* and pray for our partner or the subject of our lust. The point is, we cannot objectify, lust over, or think negatively about someone and pray for them at the same time. Fill in the blanks of this prayer for anything that satisfies the above categories:

"[Higher Power], I surrender my right to_____ (lust, objectify, think negatively about…).

I pray for them as_____ (someone's daughter, wife or future wife, sister…).

I pray for their_____ (well-being, career, growth into healthy people…).

And I ask for you to show me what I need right now and who I am in you."

Now, rewrite the prayer for yourself two ways, a) for sex addiction and b) for *negative narrative*.

a)

b)

How many times a day do you pray? How will prayer help you in your recovery?

THE FOUNDATIONS OF RECOVERY - PART 2 DIGGING DEEPER

Step 3 Connection: Prayer is a way to turn our will, passions, lusts, and desires over, surrendering our life. This is a big step. This comes with a gift of desperation for our higher power's way, not our own. Explain your desperation for a new way to live and a new way to think about others.

[ ]

PARTNER CONNECT Take a moment to write down 3 things that you appreciate about your partner. Share these with them today.

Do the Opposite

Exercise 17

Whether you're recovering from lust, sex addiction, infidelity, betrayal, or intimacy avoidant behaviors, the fact is that your life has become unmanageable. You need to change the choices and roads you used to walk on. You will need to think about the minute-by-minute, hourly, and daily choices you make. Recovery is day-to-day. Alcoholics Anonymous calls recovery "one day at a time." This is our mentality to follow the *One Path* of recovery.

You will need to think of these actions and what their opposite may be. For example:

- watch TV/MA shows vs. create an entertainment boundary
- lust over a woman jogging on the sidewalk vs. pray for her/snap your rubber band/1 second rule
- ruminate on negative thoughts about your partner vs. remind yourself of a gratitude about them
- play the victim about the patience in atonement vs. remind yourself of the responsibility you are taking

Create 10 opposites you can choose in your recovery to practice. It *is* practice. If you are struggling with thinking of more, make a call to someone in recovery and think of more to add.

Situations/Triggers/Temptations	I choose the opposite by doing…
1.	1.
2.	2.
3.	3.
4.	4.
5.	5.
6.	6.
7.	7.
8.	8.
9.	9.
10.	10.

THE FOUNDATIONS OF RECOVERY - PART 2 DIGGING DEEPER

Step 1 Connection: Which of the 10 above are you powerless over happening? Admit these and associate a feeling with each that you are powerless over.

PARTNER CONNECT With your partner, share 3 of the 10 "opposite" things that you are going to do to stay in recovery. Have you identified how you are going to keep yourself accountable for doing these things? Share your ideas for accountability with your partner.

OBJECTIFICATION

Flush the Toilet

Exercise 18

This saying is commonly associated with getting rid of harmful, damaging drugs in a desperate act of "getting rid of" the tool of your self-destruction. In sexual addiction or intimacy avoidance, flushing the toilet would be a middle circle behavior *(see the 3 Circles Exercise)* that can cut off your acting out and redirect you towards health.

It's not a matter of if but *when* you will need to "flush" a sexual temptation of lust or a negative thought about your partner. The question you must ask yourself is, "Am I desperate enough to want to completely rid my life of these destructive behaviors?" Desperation for change is a gift, a posture, a recognition of guilt. Picture your toilet. It's dirty. Taking destructive thoughts and behavior, mentally throwing them into the toilet, and choosing to flush them down is a practice, not a one-time event.

If you let negative, dirty, and/or destructive thought patterns stay in your heart, what are the outcomes?

What lustful thoughts or negative narratives about your partner are you choosing to flush?

Pick a thought you would like to flush today. How does it feel to visualize it leaving your mind and going down the toilet? Reread your *appreciation & resignation letters* associated with what you flushed.

Step 6-7 Connection: Remember each of your defects of character and write statement of flushing the toilet for each.

(Example: I surrender this _____ (sexual temptation/negative narrative), and I flush it down the toilet)

OBJECTIFICATION

Caught Looking – Real or Perceived

Exercise 19

"Our eyes betray us" is an understatement in sexual addiction recovery. Whatever the degree of sexual betrayal, when your partner suspects you were looking at an attractive woman in lust, their perception is what matters in the moment. Whether you were looking or not, their perception that you did reminded them of all the hurt associated with your sexual infidelity and betrayal. So, we *Hear and Validate* the pain they are experiencing in the moment.

- "I can tell you are in pain from _____."
- "I have hurt you in the past with ogling and lusting over other women. I am guilty of that, and I take full responsibility for that."
- Tell the Truth: "I was/wasn't looking at or lusting over that person."
- "Regardless, I have been guilty of that and I am terribly sorry for it, and it makes sense for you to feel_____."
- "What do you need from me at this moment?"

The point is, their perspective and pain must be acknowledged and met with as much empathy as you can muster. This is truly centered on humility and the surrender of defensiveness. Your ego is not what matters here, their perspective is.

Turn the tables around. Explain the pain you would feel if your partner acted out sexually with another person, and the pain you'd feel if you caught them looking at someone in lust.

Then, ask your partner to explain the feelings they'd have if they caught you looking at and lusting over another.

ALL Step Connection: Since the steps are in the context of "we," ask someone who's been in recovery longer than you what this interaction looks like. How does it look if done in a responsible way or a destructive way in their relationship? Share what it looks like in your relationship. Record what they say here, and any similarities.

[ ]

PARTNER CONNECT With your partner, be sure to share what you wrote in the "Turn the Tables Around" section before moving on to other parts of the exercise.

OBJECTIFICATION

Look Up

Exercise 20

This is a practice much like many of the tools provided in this exercise book. They are not a one-time event. Looking up can keep our focus, attention, and perspective on things greater than the shame, guilt, and destruction we have caused.

So, straighten your posture, look yourself in the eyes, and get ready!

By looking others in the eyes and then tracking our attention upward, we can practice multiple exercises while maintaining fidelity for our partner. Your partner will see where your eyes point, throughout your recovery and perhaps indefinitely. It's valid that they care where your eyes go and where you are looking. By looking up and maintaining eye contact, when necessary, you can navigate away from tempting locations in the area.

When you look up you can: pray to humanize, hear and validate, battle objectification, flush the toilet, take a breath, pause, seek a higher power's will, take a thought captive, and surrender it.

How have your eyes betrayed you, and caused destruction for your heart, your partner, and those you look at?

What benefits could you and the ones you love gain from your eyes being trained to look up?

Look into the mirror and explain your day to yourself. Hear and validate yourself for the feelings you have about the day, all while looking into your eyes and up. Practice this in the mirror and in the world for the next week.

Day #	1	2	3	4	5	6	7
Check Box							

Step 7 Connection: When an intrusive thought comes, ask your higher power to remove the defect, take it captive, speak a verse over the thought, and surrender your will – all while looking up! Reflect on the experience in the space below.

OBJECTIFICATION

Positioning

Exercise 21

Picture yourself sitting in your favorite restaurant with your partner. The booth you usually sit at was taken, so you are given a table at which your chair is facing the hall leading in and out of the kitchen. Directly in your line of sight, you see waitstaff going in and out of the kitchen. Your partner's seat, across from you, is facing other booths. Which "position" is better for you to have sat in?

The story above happens more often than we realize. We can use positioning to our advantage when strategically avoiding temptations to ogle or gaze at women passing by our view. If we can create less traffic in our peripheral view by "positioning" ourselves in a different seat, then we do so. This helps our partners feel safe and helps us in our battle against lust. The goal is to be able to focus more on our partner and not what's going on around us. To honor the relationship with our eyes.

It may be good to check your positioning at a restaurant, at work, while walking through a store, in a supermarket line, or at the beach. Think about how positioning would help you in the battle against lust.

Name the situations in which your eyes wander, and lust is a temptation. Think about daily events. Think about special events. Think about the locations that always seem to present a challenge for you.

[ ]

For each of the situations or locations above, create a plan to reposition yourself. Discuss this on a phone call with another person in recovery.

[ ]

Step 4 Connection: If you haven't done so already, add the situations or locations in which you have lusted over women to your inventory. Process each within the table provided for your inventory or in a separate journal you used for inventory.

PARTNER CONNECT With your partner, share your plan for positioning and explain why this is an important part of your recovery. Explain to them that you may occasionally need to change positions when in a crowded area like a restaurant.

OBJECTIFICATION

Eye Contact

Exercise 22

Many times, years go by when your lust and objectification over the body are the first thing you notice about a person. Your mind has been preconditioned to do this from pornography and media, and reinforced by society. We need to make a conscious choice to see a person in a different way. This begins with healthy communication with your partner and those of the opposite sex in general.

If you and your partner are sexually active at the moment, giving her eye contact will help you to see her, connect in intimacy, and keep you from objectifying her as well.

Giving eye contact while in discussion keeps your eyes from wandering down. Pair this exercise with the *look up* method and *humanize by prayer* to maximize your recovery.

When you communicate with your partner, does she appreciate your eye contact? Why do you think she does?

When and where have your eyes betrayed you? Make a list of places you'll need to prepare to maintain eye contact.

Bookend a situation this week where you will need to keep eye contact with another in recovery. Describe how it felt to keep eye contact during healthy communication.

THE FOUNDATIONS OF RECOVERY - PART 2 DIGGING DEEPER

Step 6 Connection: Are you ready to have your higher power work on your eye contact? Write a statement for why/why not.

PARTNER CONNECT Share with your partner what you wrote about why you think they appreciate eye contact. Do they agree with what you wrote? Ask them if they have any additional input. Write down what they say.

OBJECTIFICATION

One Second

Exercise 23

The moment you notice an attraction towards someone other than your spouse, look away! This exercise is simple when it stands alone. The longer you look, the longer you are drinking lust and fueling fantasy for your sex addicted mind. Your brain will crave another look, but you will have to practice doing the opposite of what you want. This is the destructive habit of rubbernecking that many sex addicts battle with.

Pairing this exercise with others can be helpful such as *flushing the toilet, doing the opposite,* and *humanizing with prayer*. By choosing something else for your mind to focus on, you're choosing to be in recovery and to be free from the temptation of lust.

Prayer can be especially useful in an instant.

Recall the first two parts of the *Humanize by Prayer* exercise:

"I surrender my right to_____ (lust, objectify, think negatively about…).

I pray for them as_____ (someone's daughter, wife or future wife, sister…)."

Write these two lines of prayer in your own words.

Name a time, place, and situation where you "looked too long" and lusted when your partner was with you.

How will your partner benefit from you being faithful with your eyes?

THE FOUNDATIONS OF RECOVERY - PART 2 DIGGING DEEPER

Step 4 Connection: Using the time and place named above, describe the reason why it is wrong to gawk at and lust over someone. Add this to your inventory.

[ ]

PARTNER CONNECT Once you have completed the exercise, ask your partner to share how they feel when you look too long at other people. Write down what they say.

OBJECTIFICATION

Don't Use Your Partner to Masturbate

Exercise 24

When first entering sexual addiction recovery, someone who has been in a program for a very, very long time said, "don't use your wife to masturbate with."

Why do you think someone would say that?

When somebody gets into sexual addiction recovery and they're used to sexual release on a regular basis to pornography or acting out with other people, it's very common for them to turn to their partner for their consistent sexual relief.

They will begin to project the porn they have viewed onto their wife.

This may not sound bad, except that you're engaging with your wife or partner not to connect with them in sexual intimacy, but for sexual release.

That means that you're treating your partner like an object, and that's anti-relational and destructive.

Think of a time when you objectified your partner and saw her solely as a sexual release. How would she feel about you treating her this way?

Now, to counter the objectification, list out **at least 5 things** that you cherish about your partner. This is called humanization. These are ways that you see her value, identity, and worth in who she is and her character.

Step 4 Connection: Being sexually used is a harm that will go unnoticed and unconfessed unless you do the work to uncover your patterns of acting out. Name a time you have "used" your partner sexually and what you selfishly gained out of doing it.

THE FOUNDATIONS OF RECOVERY - PART 2 DIGGING DEEPER

PARTNER CONNECT Share the 5 things you wrote down about what you cherish about your partner with them. Do not share any other parts of this exercise with your partner, as it will likely cause them pain to hear how you have objectified and used them.

Helping Your Partner Heal
(Part 2)

Exercise 25 — Wounding Agent vs Healing Agent

This exercise is specifically helpful in conflict. As guys, even though we may seem ok with conflict, we truly don't want to have conflict in a relationship.

We also call this the **two choices tool**. Re-wounding agent vs Healing Agent.

Re-wounding Agent: What are we saying or doing that is: destructive, hurtful, holding back the growth? (We do these things to make ourselves feel safe)

Healing Agent: What am I doing or saying that is helpful and helping the other person feel safe?

Every time we are in conflict, we have this choice. We can still be a Healing Agent and get our point across to the other person.

Reflect on what you are **saying or doing** (or avoiding doing) that is either Re-Wounding or Healing your relationships. List at least 7 for each.

Re-Wounding	Healing

Step 8/9 Connection: Use this list of Re-Wounding actions and cross-reference your steps 8/9 to see if there are any places you may need to include in your amends to those you have harmed. Write a prayer below to open your heart to giving amends for these ways you have been Re-Wounding others in conflict.

PARTNER CONNECT Share what you are learning in this exercise with your partner. Ask them for their input. Write down what they say and use it to complete the exercise.

HELPING YOUR PARTNER HEAL (PART 2)

Coercive Sex - Cup of Tea

Exercise 26

Have you heard of the *cup of tea* analogy for sexual engagement? When you read "tea," equate that with sex.

It goes like this: you ask your partner if they would like a cup of tea. If they say yes, great, make them tea. If they say no, then don't.

Then, if they wanted tea, you may go heat the water, prepare the tea, and bring it to them, BUT

What if they say they now don't want a cup of tea?

Then don't make them drink it. Don't get annoyed. Now they don't want it. They have their own choice and that's ok for them to change it.

If they are unconscious, don't make them drink tea. They may have said yes earlier, BUT

It's taken too long to get the tea ready. Set the tea down, leave it for another day/time.

If they started drinking the tea and passed out while drinking it, don't keep pouring it down their throat.

If they wanted to drink tea last Saturday, that doesn't mean they want it every night.

If you can understand how ridiculous it is to expect or force someone else to drink tea.

It's the same with consent in sex. It's ok to say "no" and to be told "no" to.

When your partner says no to you, is it ok with you? Why should it be ok?

| |
| |

In what ways do you "prepare" the tea? Your partner needs to feel emotionally safe throughout the day to want to have sex. What ways can you choose to do that? Ask others in recovery how they create emotional safety for their partner.

| |
| |

What is your initiation statement? What do you say to your partner to offer tea? Write 1 or 2 sentences below that offer yourself sexually. Be ok with their "no." Say the sentences to yourself in the mirror.

| |
| |

Step 9 Connection: In your sexual addiction inventory of harms done to others, consider if you have ever been coercive with sex. Have you pressured, complained, or been entitled about sex? What about with your partner? Complete an inventory entry for coercion and add it to your amends in step 9.

THE FOUNDATIONS OF RECOVERY - PART 2 DIGGING DEEPER

Subject: Coercive Sex	What Happened	My Reaction	My Reason

PARTNER CONNECT Consult with your partner regarding your initiation statement. Ask them if this is an okay way to approach them, or if they would prefer something different. Take note of what they say.

Drama Triangle

Exercise 27

Drama refers to the feelings we have that are born from a physical, emotional, and spiritual need. Every person has a way that they will fall into drama with their partner. Stress induces the beginning of our role. Here are the 3 roles and ways to get out of them.

Rescuer: This is the desire to help someone, but it gets twisted to actually taking control of the situation. This is the "Mr. Fix It" persona. You may feel like, if you don't fix it, there is something wrong with you (shame) or you will be guilty of not having a solution to a problem.

Ways out: An example of how to get out of this role is to express understanding (see the Understanding Exercise). Encouraging the other person to seek a solution is a healthier alternative to providing one for them.

Persecutor: This persona will come out as critical, angry, and putting the other person down. Whether this is verbally or in your heart, this is destructive to the relationship.

Ways out: Be willing to listen to the other person and surrender the negative narrative you tell yourself about your partner. Take responsibility for your own actions, tone, demeanor, and words.

Victim: This role is a state of helplessness, powerlessness, and feeling misunderstood. Many traumas and wrongs committed towards us in our lives can give us an excuse to stay in this role or even act this role as a form of safety.

Ways out: Confess your victim mindset to another. Return to a state of thinking positively about yourself and others. Write down and express gratitude for what is true about yourself and your partner.

Which role do you sometimes take? Why?

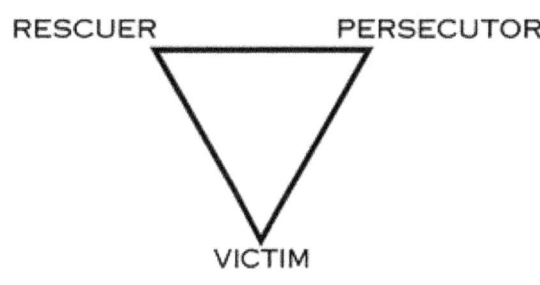

Which role does your partner sometimes take? Why?

For your recovery, what actions can you take to exit your role and return to a place of love for your partner?

[ ]

Step 10 Connection: Use opportunities throughout this week to make any amends necessary to you causing drama in your relationship. Record such instances here.

[ ]

PARTNER CONNECT You may share this exercise with your partner. Be cautious in sharing ways you think your partner participates in the Drama Triangle. It may be best to ask them about how they see their part.

HELPING YOUR PARTNER HEAL (PART 2)

Time Out Protocol

Exercise 28

The Time Out Protocol is the final piece of the three-part Communication Plan. There may be occasions when one or both partners become overwhelmed with emotions to the point that they can't function in a way that will support the health of the relationship. When someone is flooded with emotion, they may say or do things that attack the other person—adding even more pain to an already painful situation.

As a countermeasure to overwhelming emotions, the couple should develop a code word or a non-verbal sign that is an indicator that one of them needs to stop talking before they do more damage than good. Once a code word is spoken or a non-verbal sign is shown, the couple will disengage and agree to come back at a later time when things have calmed down. The couple should agree to the terms of time-out ahead of time and consider the Time Out Plan to be a contract between the two parties.

There are 5 main points to keep in mind when considering whether or not to call a time out:

1. USE THE CODE WORD or NON-VERBAL SIGN SPARINGLY. Time-outs are considered an emergency option when all attempts at productive communication have failed. Understand that if either partner uses their code word or non-verbal sign to get out of conversations that they just don't want to deal with, they are hurting their partner. Using the code word or non-verbal sign to stonewall is also an improper use of a time-out.

2. The request for time out should be honored. One partner should not try to goad the other into reengaging. The conversation needs to stop when time out is called. No attempting to have the last word.

3. When a code word or non-verbal sign has been used, agree on a time to reengage. Otherwise, one or both partners could feel neglected and abandoned. Typically, 20-30 minutes is recommended for a time-out.

4. When a time-out is taken, we recommend that each person practice self-care. This means that an activity should be done to take the mind OFF of the present problem, as opposed to taking the time to stew about it and/or plan a rebuttal. Reading a book (not on the subject of the argument or infidelity), taking a shower/bath, or taking a walk are great activities to do. Time-outs do not work if either party uses the time to sit around and think about how angry they are or what they are going to say next to win the argument. The idea is to take your mind completely off the argument and give your flooded system a break.

5. When you come back from the time out, each partner needs to state at least one thing they appreciate about the other before resuming the conversation. When sharing feelings, use "I feel" statements as opposed to "you" statements. "You" statements come off as blaming. Blaming and/or criticizing will only make the problem worse. Focus on the solution as opposed to the problem(s) and be good listeners.

As with the Trigger Plan, the Time Out Plan should be developed at a calm moment.

To Do:

SIGN A COMMITMENT WITH YOUR PARTNER. FOR THE NEXT 90 DAYS, YOU WILL TRY USING THIS

And return to this exercise to check if completed

PARTNER CONNECT Stonewalling is highly damaging to relationships. Identify at least two times in the past when you have stonewalled your partner. How did this damage your relationship? Ask them how this hurt them and write down what they say. Share your commitment to not use the Time Out Protocol to stonewall your partner when you don't feel like having a conversation. Commit to coming back to the conversation after the agreed-upon time has elapsed.

Demeanor Part 2

Exercise 29

If you are a wounding partner reading this and your partner is continuing to emotionally flood, chances are that you are engaging in behavior that is causing them to feel unsafe.

If you cannot or will not do everything you can to create a safe environment for your partner, any advances toward the restoration of the relationship will be slow to non-existent.

If you do not know what it is that you need to do, you should ask your partner at a time when they are not emotionally flooded. Typically, the things that make a wounded partner feel most safe are prioritizing the relationship, accountability for your actions and whereabouts, your availability to listen to them and meet their needs, and the consistency with which you behave in a manner that they interpret as loving.

Ask your partner and return here to reflect on their response and requests.

However, your partner may have other requirements. If these requirements are reasonable, agree to meet them. If you are not sure if they are reasonable, engage the help of a trained professional to help you understand.

As the wounding partner, earning back trust will require a great deal of patience on your part. You may tell your partner time and time again that you are "all in," but it takes much more than words to prove to them that you mean it. Rushing your partner toward "recovery" by complaining about their need to talk about it or shutting them down is not only unfair and inappropriate, but it comes across as controlling and uncaring.

You need to remember that their reactions are in response to your deception. It is going to take quite a while before they believe that you are no longer engaged in a double life. A word of caution: we see many wounding partners, especially intimacy avoidants, insist that their partner stop bringing the infidelity up in conversation. This will backfire if you are at all interested in the restoration of trust in the relationship.

Wounded partners who are shut down in this way share with us that they continue to feel a profound lack of trust and safety, even if they aren't voicing it. The only thing that shutting the conversation down does is ensure that the wounded partner does not share their feelings with you. This erodes trust even further over the long run and often results in the relationship ending.

Reflect:

Turn back to Demeanor Part 1. What actions have you been consistent in, inconsistent in, or need to begin to create safety for your partner?

THE FOUNDATIONS OF RECOVERY - PART 2 DIGGING DEEPER

Consistent	
Inconsistent	
Need to Begin	

Consistent	
Inconsistent	
Need to Begin	

Consistent	
Inconsistent	
Need to Begin	

Consistent	
Inconsistent	
Need to Begin	

Consistent	
Inconsistent	
Need to Begin	

Consistent	
Inconsistent	
Need to Begin	

The Cynical Script

Exercise 30

Our cynical script is the story that we tell ourselves that gives us the excuse or the reason not to connect or to stay disconnected from our partner.

This is what we tell ourselves that gives us justification to create distance, or stay distant, from our partner.

List 5 lies or negative stories you tell yourself about your partner below:

1. _____
2. _____
3. _____
4. _____
5. _____

If we have a cynical script of our partner, then we're looking at them like they're a problem. We're looking at the negative part about them. We're looking at where they fall short of the narrative that we create. The cynical script says they are a certain way, they're going to stay a certain way, and that they're against us.

We must rewrite the cynical script. One way to do it is gratitude.

List 5 gratitudes you have about your partner below:

1. _____
2. _____
3. _____
4. _____
5. _____

Tip: Snap your rubber band when a cynical script comes into your mind and pray gratitude in your heart.

Step 10 Connection: Compare your cynical scripts and gratitudes with a recovery partner. Pray with one another over the phone, for help to express gratitude instead of cynicism.

PARTNER CONNECT Do not share this exercise with your partner, as it will likely cause them pain.

Apology Language

Exercise 31

Much like the well-known "Love Languages," we also have ways in which we would prefer to be apologized to when our partner has hurt us.

Your partner has a preferred way for you to make amends to them. Your partner needs to know that you fully understand the hurt you have caused and what was broken in that hurt.

Here are the 5 apology languages:

1. Expressing Regret	Using the words "I am sorry for…I regret hurting you by doing…"
2. Accepting Responsibility	Saying, "I was wrong. _____ was wrong to do to you. I take full responsibility for my actions."
3. Make Restitution	Asking, "What can I do right now to make it right?" If it's reasonable, do it.
4. Genuinely Repenting	Stating that you will work on it and being specific in what actions will be evidence of success or failure.
5. Requesting Forgiveness	Humbling yourself and admitting you're wrong with an invitation of "will you forgive me?"

Rank in order the 5 apology languages. This will show you how some ways of communication in an apology mean more to you. So, write **why** you would appreciate each form of an apology.

1._____ Why…_____
_____

2._____ Why…_____
_____

3._____ Why…_____
_____

4._____ Why…_____
_____

5._____ Why…_____
_____

ALL Step Connection: Share your apology languages with a recovery partner to prepare for sharing them with your partner. Reflect below on why it would be important to know your partner's apology language.

PARTNER CONNECT Once you have crafted your apology letter, with the help of a recovery partner, share it with your partner.

Reparations

Exercise 32

This is where we say that our actions speak louder than words ever can. Creating your list of reparations for your partner is an exercise in all the ways that you are repaying them for the pain you have caused with your SA/PA/IA behaviors. For this exercise, refer to the top 10 IA behaviors you have completed earlier in this exercise book AND your boundaries to remain sexually sober from your addiction of acting out.

Fill out the two tables below. The reparation/consequence actions are your ongoing responsibility for maintaining connection to your partner.

IA example: Action/Behavior is avoiding conflict around topics → Your reparation is to use the empathy exercise to hear her pain for 4 nights a week.

SA/PA example: Action/Behavior is purposefully looking at sexually stimulating images → Reparation is one week of sleeping on the couch after massages for your partner nightly.

IA Action/Behavior	Reparation

SA/PA Action/Behavior	Reparation

Step 8 Connection: Write a prayer around becoming willing to make amends. This prayer must include acknowledgement to your higher power of the pain you have caused and continue to cause your partner. Surrender your life to your higher power to heal, repair, and reconcile your relationship.

PARTNER CONNECT Share what you're working on with your partner. Ask them about actions they consider especially meaningful that will help you make amends. Do this before completing the exercise.

Love Language Sandwich   Exercise 33

The 5 love languages were first developed by Gary Chapman. They are...

1. Acts of Service
2. Receiving Gifts
3. Quality Time
4. Words of Affirmation
5. Physical Touch

These have been researched, used, and proven in practice for years in relationships. The goal of this exercise is to discover your partner's current top two love languages. Use this link to have your partner take a quiz.
https://5lovelanguages.com/quizzes

My partner's top two love languages are _____ and _____.

What would prevent you from accommodating these love languages?

[ ]

Make a commitment in your marathon of recovery to fulfill one of the top two languages in the morning, and the other at night.

Brainstorm some ideas for how you can show each language to your partner. You can search for ways online, ask another person in recovery, or have a conversation with your partner and ask them.

Love Language #1: _____	Love Language #2: _____
IDEAS: • • • • •	IDEAS: • • • •

Now, rewrite which of them can be shown to your partner in the morning and which can be shown at night.

AM	PM
• • • • •	• • • •

THE FOUNDATIONS OF RECOVERY - PART 2 DIGGING DEEPER

Step 11 Connection: Recovery is a marathon. Write a prayer asking your higher power to open your heart to show love with authenticity.

[   ]

I, _____, commit to showing my partner, _____, love for the next 90 days using the following page to keep track.

Signature_____ Date_____

Check the boxes for each day you showed your partner love.

1	2	3	4	5	6	7	8	9	10
11	12	13	14	15	16	17	18	19	20
21	22	23	24	25	26	27	28	29	30
31	32	33	34	35	36	37	38	39	40
41	42	43	44	45	46	47	48	49	50
51	52	53	54	55	56	57	58	59	60
61	62	63	64	65	66	67	68	69	70
71	72	73	74	75	76	77	78	79	80
81	82	83	84	85	86	87	88	89	90

Importance of Dates

Exercise 34

Weekly dates are essential for building and keeping a strong relationship. In Bradford Wilcox and Jeffery Dew's study "The Date Night Opportunity: What Does Couple Time Tell Us About the Potential Value of Date Nights?" There are 5 reasons to make time for weekly dates.

1. <u>Good Communication</u>: On dates, you want to practice having open communication. It must be viewed as something you are always improving in.
2. <u>Novelty</u>: Doing something new with your partner can create excitement and fresh memories in the relationship.
3. <u>Romantic Love</u>: This is the aspect that can spark a memory of why you fell in love and the things that you're grateful for about your partner.
4. <u>Commitment</u>: By consistently planning dates, you will grow closer in trust and accountability for nurturing the relationship.
5. <u>Destress</u>: Making memories and having fun can be a much-needed break from discussion about the hard topics such as infidelity, sex addiction, and intimacy avoidance.

Suggestion: You alternate who decides where and what you will do on the date. This gives both partners the chance to plan new and different things for the two of you to have fun doing together.

Pitfalls: Last minute planning, dates you know your partner won't enjoy, being busy or distracted on the date, being inconsistent in planning dates every week, and of course sex addiction behaviors such as ogling or flirting can re-wound your partner (See *Battling Objectification* for SA tips).

Which of the 5 reasons are you the weakest in? Why?

Which of the pitfalls have you fallen into? Recall how it made your partner feel for each.

Come up with ideas and plan for dates over the next 13 weeks. Identify different places to eat and enjoy a fun activity. Call others in recovery for ideas. Research places to eat.

Week	Food	Activity	Date
1			__/__/__
2			__/__/__
3			__/__/__
4			__/__/__
5			__/__/__
6			__/__/__
7			__/__/__
8			__/__/__
9			__/__/__
10			__/__/__
11			__/__/__
12			__/__/__
13			__/__/__

Step 2 Connection: Write a prayer expressing your desire for your relationship to grow and heal, mentioning dates as a way to do so.

Warning Signs

SA/PA Warning Signs

Exercise 35

Since recovery is an ongoing process, you will need to be vigilant in what you think, say, do, and believe. Every thought can lead to a path of action. Every belief will manifest in some way in your relationships.

Instructions

On the left-hand side of the table, list the attitudes, thoughts, behaviors, and beliefs that are warning signs to you that you might be headed for a relapse into sexually addictive behavior or pornography use. On the right-hand side, write down strategies for coping with these.

Attitudes, Thoughts, Behaviors, and Beliefs *Warning Signs*	Strategies to Cope

THE FOUNDATIONS OF RECOVERY - PART 2 DIGGING DEEPER

WARNING SIGNS

Price of Addiction

Exercise 36

In this exercise, we will focus in on the time, energy, and ultimately financial cost of your sexual addiction.

The purpose of doing this is to reveal just how much your addiction has cost you.

Age Range	Acting Out Behaviors	Hours in Behavior Weekly	Your Average Hourly Wage	Total Price of Addiction
5-10				
11-20				
21-30				
31-40				
41-50				
51-60				
61-70				
71-80				
80+				

Total Weekly Hours [ ]   Price Of Addiction [ ]

Miscellaneous Costs

Legal Fees _____
Therapy _____
Child
Support _____
Other

_____ _____

_____ _____

Total Price Of Addiction [ ]

THE FOUNDATIONS OF RECOVERY - PART 2 DIGGING DEEPER

Step 5 Connection: Confess the cost to another in recovery. List the feelings you have about the price of your addiction here. Then, write the price and time lost on a flash card and place it into your wallet where you keep cash and cards.

Tips to Avoid Relapse

Exercise 37

Here we prepare our recovery journey for all the situations where we'll be tempted to act out in our sexual addiction.

For everything from mental fantasy to paid sex, you can set up plans to avoid temptations. Each section below has three lines, but use more if you need to. Remember: temptation is a powerless thing, but the choice to run from your addiction is in your power.

1. **Cravings are temporary.** Distract yourself with activities or make phone calls until the cravings pass.

   a.

   b.

2. **Don't think you have it beat.** It isn't uncommon for people to relapse after years of sobriety if they become complacent or make excuses like, "one time won't hurt me."

   a.

   b.

3. **Avoid risky situations.** Avoid risky situations, such as not having adequate blocking software, using your phone late at night, or watching visually stimulating movies or videos—even if they aren't "technically" pornography.

   a.

   b.

4. **Remember relapse doesn't start with off-limits behavior.** Relapse starts to happen the moment you make excuses that put yourself in risky situations. This is usually long before you act out. Many addicts report having relapsed after they were "riding the line" for days or weeks.

   a.

   b.

THE FOUNDATIONS OF RECOVERY - PART 2 DIGGING DEEPER

5. **Don't view relapse as a complete failure.** If you slip up, own it. Don't use it as an excuse to fall back into old patterns.

a.

b.

Step 1 Connection: You may be powerless over the temptations to relapse, although there are day-to-day choices that you have power over. What choices will you make to avoid relapse this week?

PARTNER CONNECT With your partner, share the activities you have identified to fight cravings. Who are you going to be accountable to?

IA Warning Signs

Exercise 38

Since recovery is an ongoing process, you will need to be vigilant in what you think, say, do, and believe. Every thought can lead to a path of action. Every belief will manifest in some way in your relationships.

Instructions

On the left-hand side of the table, list the attitudes, thoughts, behaviors, and beliefs that are warning signs to you that you might be headed for a relapse into IA behavior. On the right-hand side, write down strategies for coping with these.

Attitudes, Thoughts, Behaviors, and Beliefs *Warning Signs*	Strategies to Cope

THE FOUNDATIONS OF RECOVERY - PART 2 DIGGING DEEPER

PARTNER CONNECT Ask your partner for their input on your IA warning signs.

How to Spot IA Behaviors   Exercise 39

A big question we get is: "How do I know if the behavior I'm experiencing is related to IA?"

Not every behavior is related to IA.

We all have bad days.

There are 6 questions that you can ask that help determine whether it was IA or not:

1. Was this behavior directed at the partner only? If so, what was I feeling?
2. Was the behavior effective at creating distance? If so, in which way?
3. Do I use this behavior repetitively? If so, how often per week?
4. Did the behavior move us closer together or further apart? If so, in what ways?
5. Did the behavior occur after sexual, emotional, or spiritual connection? If so, explain.
6. When confronted by the behavior, did the IA analyze the situation or grow defensive?

Over the course of the next week be mindful of your behaviors. Recall that there are 40 types of behaviors of IA, which we have given you in a previous exercise. In the table below, analyze your behavior using the 6 questions above.

Behavior: _____

1. _____
   _____
2. _____
   _____
3. _____
   _____
4. _____
   _____
5. _____
   _____
6. _____
   _____

THE FOUNDATIONS OF RECOVERY - PART 2 DIGGING DEEPER

Behavior: _____

1. _____
   _____
2. _____
   _____
3. _____
   _____
4. _____
   _____
5. _____
   _____
6. _____
   _____

Behavior: _____

1. _____
   _____
2. _____
   _____
3. _____
   _____
4. _____
   _____
5. _____
   _____
6. _____
   _____

Step 11 Connection: Write a prayer and surrender the thoughts, feelings, and subsequent behaviors you still struggle with. Open your heart in honesty and dependency for your higher power's help.

Middle of the Roof

Exercise 40

Have you ever stood on a roof? Anyone who has, knows the safest place to stand is at the peak with a foot on either side. Picture this analogy for your recovery. There are actions, behaviors, and temptations that would be considered "edging," walking towards the edge of the roof. If we aren't careful, they will lead to relapse or avoiding intimacy with our partners. Our goal in recovery is to stay in the "middle of the roof." Falling off the roof would be harmful towards yourself and others.

There are aspects of our lives that are in our control and others that are out of our control.

Identifying the actions, behaviors, and temptations for both are essential to staying in the "middle of the roof."

Examples:

In your control: what you watch for entertainment, what you eat/drink, when you go to bed, making a phone call, where you drive, who you spend your time with, how you manage your stress (*self-care plan*)

Not in your control: your thoughts, other's perspectives/opinions of you or in general, your feelings, your memories, your past

What actions, behaviors, or temptations walk you towards the edge and eventually falling off the roof?

Organize these into the table below:

In your control	Not in your control

How does your partner feel when you "edge" towards relapse in SA or avoid intimacy? How would you and your partner benefit from your recovery in these areas?

THE FOUNDATIONS OF RECOVERY - PART 2 DIGGING DEEPER

Step 1 Connection: Over a phone call, share the things out of your control with another person in recovery.

Record similarities you both share in the space below.

PARTNER CONNECT In order to complete your assignment, you need to ask your partner about how they feel when you engage in behaviors that "edge" you toward relapse. Also, ask them how they would benefit from your recovery in these areas. Record their answers.

Anger and Resentment Letter — Exercise 41

We all have anger and resentment. Most of us have heard the expression, "resentment is like drinking poison and expecting the other person to die." We know that resentment is corrosive by nature, both personally and relationally. It's time to process this so we're not carrying it around. Here's a way to do that.

You're going to write a one-to-two-page letter, expressing your intense and specific anger, resentment, frustration, etc. This isn't *dear honey*. This is sharing all the things that they've done to you, ways they've hurt you or caused you pain. When we're resentful, we hold onto and focus on situations out of context. In this exercise, you're just going to write what you dwell on in anger outside of context so that you can really get it out.

You will write separate anger letters toward the areas below. List out your resentments for each before their letters.

1. Wounded Partner
2. Yourself
3. Mother &/or Father
4. God/Higher Power

1. Anger/Resentment towards partner

[   ]

2. Anger/Resentment towards yourself

[   ]

THE FOUNDATIONS OF RECOVERY - PART 2 DIGGING DEEPER

3. Anger/Resentment towards mom and dad

4. Anger/Resentment towards God/Higher Power

WARNING SIGNS

I write this to **express my anger/resentment towards** _____

I write this to **express my anger/resentment towards** _____

WARNING SIGNS

I write this to **express my anger/resentment towards** _____

I write this to **express my anger/resentment towards** _____

Releasing Anger and Resentment

Exercise 42

After you're done with your letters, you are going to take each resentment, frustration, etc., line by line and break it apart.

You will break apart all of your letters into sentence statements for each of the following:

a. The picture (What specific memory or image comes to your mind?)
b. The movie (What does the scene look like? What is the context of the anger? Why?)
c. The truth (Describe the conflict)
d. What you're going to do to let it go (Action sentence)
e. How are you going to release it emotionally?
f. How are you going to release it through physical activity? (explain)

Anger/Resentment Towards Partner	
The picture	
The movie	
The truth	
What you're going to do to let it go	
How are you going to release it emotionally?	
How are you going to release it through physical activity?	

Anger/Resentment Towards Yourself	
The picture	
The movie	
The truth	
What you're going to do to let it go	

How are you going to release it emotionally?	
How are you going to release it through physical activity?	

Anger/Resentment Towards Mom/Dad	
The picture	
The movie	
The truth	
What you're going to do to let it go	
How are you going to release it emotionally?	
How are you going to release it through physical activity?	

Anger/Resentment Towards God/Higher Power	
The picture	
The movie	
The truth	
What you're going to do to let it go	
How are you going to release it emotionally?	
How are you going to release it through physical activity?	

WARNING SIGNS

Step 7 Connection: In order to be prepared to ask God/Higher Power to remove our character defects, we must be honest. This is especially true about anger/resentment. Let the walls come down. You are accepted even if you feel anger. Share this anger with another this week and pray together over it. Reflect on the way it felt to be honest to your higher power and a person about this anger.

Exercise 43 — Affair Types

<u>The One Night Stand</u> – opportunity and convenience. If this was you then you need to set boundaries with business, with other women, and with travel. Identify a good peer group that has the same values.

- This results in loose boundaries
  - Carelessness is involved
- Pride
- Alcohol

<u>Love Struck</u> – This is the limerence affair. You think that you are in love and are willing to give up everything that is important to you for this infatuation. Your thinking is distorted in terms of who the affair partner was and who your partner really is.

- Obsession – pursuit of happiness that takes over everything
- In your Life Plan you have an obligation to stay committed, and you have goals that are really important to you.
- Obviously, you need to terminate the relationship.
- The third choice is about choosing your higher power over the affair partner and your spouse.
  - How do you have a life of meaning and purpose beyond just seeking happiness?
  - *31 Reasons* is a good resource

<u>Sexual Addiction</u> – this is a physiological, chemical, and escalating condition. If there is a hint that you have an addiction, then assume that that is the case. Do the 12 steps. This will keep you from relapse.

- Where you are weak you can be strong. You will have deeper relationships than you thought possible with the mentor/support community
- If you are an addict, you will 100% relapse
- Work a strong recovery program into your Life Plan
  - Give back to others who struggle with this addiction.

<u>Wanting Your Cake & Eating It Too</u> – this is more about entitlement and possibly cultural. Maybe family members did it and you have a "that's just the way things are done" mentality

- In your Life Plan, do your own work on personal integrity. Find a community of people who want to be monogamous and faithful. Don't hang out with peers who think it is ok to have an affair.

<u>Emotional Affair</u> – you look to another person to fulfill your emotional goals. You let someone else into your marriage life.

- "we are just friends" – if this is hurting the boundary around your marriage, it needs to end.
- In your Life Plan, make these kinds of relationships not an option. Make your marriage your priority.
  - Find appropriate places to get those emotional needs met.
  - Emotional affairs are just physical affairs waiting to happen.
  - What habits and ways of being do you need to change?

WARNING SIGNS

Love Addiction: you become attached to them without even knowing them. You compulsively continue to involve yourself in relationships that aren't good for you.

- SLAA – Sex and Love Addicts Anonymous

Think about what needs to be in your life plan to stay faithful.

Let's do what is necessary to protect you and your family from future hurt.

```
┌─────────────────────────────────────────────────────────┐
│                                                         │
│                                                         │
│                                                         │
│                                                         │
└─────────────────────────────────────────────────────────┘
```

Step 7 Connection: **Write a letter as if it's 5 years from now: "How I relapsed."** Explain how an affair would likely occur. Include the pain it would cause all parties involved. Finish it with a prayer asking for protection from any future affairs.

_____
_____
_____
_____
_____
_____
_____
_____
_____
_____
_____
_____
_____
_____
_____
_____

PARTNER CONNECT Share what you wrote about the steps necessary to ensure safety with your partner. Ask for their input in case you missed anything. Write down what they tell you.

Exercise 44 — Cascade Towards Betrayal

Here we will look at a list of situations, conflicts, and evidence that show a relationship is headed towards betrayal. Because many of those using this exercise book have already committed a betrayal, much of this exercise should cause you to feel guilt. This guiltiness is meant to help you come out of hiding, and recove from the very nature of your brokenness, and be honest.

Between the 1st step (turning away from or against your partner) and crossing the line to infidelity at the 20th step (Not dismissing alternative relationships), we find that Intimacy Avoidants will get all the way to step 19. Betrayal is happening even if it doesn't cross over into an inappropriate relationship with someone other than our partner.

Below, **circle** which of the 24 steps in the Cascade Towards Betrayal evidence that are a part of your story.

(1) Turning Away or Against	(2) Partner: "Not there for me"	(3) Flooding/ Physiological Arousal	(4) Conflict with repair no longer working
(5) Avoidance of Conflict, then Blowups	(6) Keeping Secrets from Others	(7) Negative Comparisons between Partner and others	(8) Attempts to Connect Decline
(9) Investment in Relationship Declines	(10) Confiding in Others, not the Partner	(11) Less Sacrificial for Relationship	(12) Maximizing Negative traits of Partner
(13) Minimizing Positive Traits of Partner	(14) Trashing on instead of Cherishing	(15) Slandering Partner	(16) Practicing Resentment v. Gratitude
(17) Loneliness in Relationship	(18) Little to no Sexuality, romance, fun, play or courtship	(19) Less Pro-Relationship Thoughts	(20) Not dismissing alternative relationships
(21) Walls with partner, Windows with others	(22) Keeping more and more Secrets from Partner	(23) Actively Turning towards others Emotionally	(24) Crossing Boundaries, Real betrayal unfolds

Gottman-Rusbult-Glass

In another color, identify any evidence that you've still been displaying lately. What are you valuing more than the relationship for 3 of these (Step 4 Connection)?

Evidence	What am I valuing more than the relationship?
1.	
2.	

PARTNER CONNECT Be sure to share what you have identified with your partner. If they have identified other evidence that you weren't aware of, write down what they say.

Marathon of Recovery

Self-Care Plan

Exercise 45

Your recovery from SA or IA is highly affected by what you do on a day-to-day basis. This exercise is meant to create a space for you to explore the actions and activities you can take, starting today, to keep yourself in a healthy mindset for yourself, your family, your friends, and above all others, your higher power. Three lines are available for each section but don't stop with just 3. Create a plan for taking care of your heart, mind, body, and spirit.

1. Activities that support my physical well-being

   a.

   b.

2. Activities that support my spiritual well-being

   a.

   b.

3. Activities that support my emotional/mental well-being

   a.

   b.

4. Activities that support my social well-being

   a.

   b.

5. Activities that support my active recovery

   a.

   b.

THE FOUNDATIONS OF RECOVERY - PART 2 DIGGING DEEPER

ALL Step Connection: Make 3 phone calls and record ideas below from their self-care plans. We are stronger together in recovery.

| 1. | 2. | 3. |

Self-Care Schedule

Exercise 46

Use your self-care worksheet to plan and create a schedule of activities, the days you will do them, and times.

Be diligent with these plans and on the same page with your partner. This can involve times when you need a quiet space to center yourself after a long day at work, exercise, prayer, and family activities, to name a few. Agree with your partner on durations of anything you plan to do without them on your own.

Activity	Day	Time

THE FOUNDATIONS OF RECOVERY - PART 2 DIGGING DEEPER

ALL Step Connection: *Bookend* these self-care activities over phone calls. With your recovery partners, share your ideas and ask them what they do for self-care.

Flawed and Loved

Exercise 47

Throughout the rest of your recovery journey, you will have times when you will doubt if you are worth being loved after all the pain you have caused. This is a flawed, broken, and shameful reaction to memories and mistakes on a weekly basis.

This exercise is meant to keep your heart free from the shame and doubts you have about being loved by your partner. It is understandable to feel those feelings, yet they are a counter against your openness and intimacy with your partner.

Here's the exercise we would like you to do with your partner.

1. Sit in chairs facing one another. Give eye contact. Clear your mind. Hold hands.
2. Say, "I am flawed."
3. Partner replies, "and I love you."
4. Repeat for 1 minute
5. Rest for 15-30 seconds
6. Repeat Steps 2-5 for a second time
7. Repeat Steps 2-5 a third time
8. Give each other a hug and kiss if comfortable.

In the table below, record your feelings after each time you use this exercise in the next week.

Repeat this exercise specifically when you are feeling like you are unlovable.

Day	Your Feelings	Your Partner's Feelings
1		
2		
3		
4		
5		
6		
7		

Step 11 Connection: Write a prayer giving up the shame and lies that you are unlovable. Accept your brokenness. Accept your heart's need to be opened and softened to receive love.

PARTNER CONNECT Ask your partner if they are open to doing this exercise with you. If they are, practice it every day with them.

Daily 10ᵗʰ Step Inventory

Exercise 48

These next two pages are meant to be printed and filled out throughout the marathon of recovery you are now entering. The point of the final 3 steps is that it's not over with. Our brokenness is only mended over a lifetime. For most of us, most of our lives have already been spent in either a sexual/porn addiction and/or intimacy avoidance. Here we will have no step connection at the end because this entire exercise can be cross-referenced with the questions you answer in the 10ᵗʰ step.

General Recovery

Resentments?

Anger?

Contempt towards

- Partner:
- Other family member:
- Other family member:
- Colleague:

Dishonesty with myself? Others?

Fear?

Gratitude list for today?

- Partner:
- Other family member:
- Other family member:
- Colleague:

New understandings/insights?

My SA/IA program

What were lust-based decisions I made?

What recovery-based decisions are people making in my SA program?

Love Language sandwich (AM- _____ 1ˢᵗ love language, (PM- _____ 2ⁿᵈ love language?

Replace these with some of the 40 ways, or from our new list

Am I busy, choosing work over my relationship?

Blame shifting?

Defending/explaining?

Playing the victim?

THE FOUNDATIONS OF RECOVERY - PART 2 DIGGING DEEPER

Expecting others to read my mind?

The Cynical Script

% Choose Door B - Self regulate, good people, boundary, what can I do for them?

Did I do bookwork?

Did I do an SA/IA meeting in the last seven days?

Did I make a recovery phone call or texts?

Did I do dailies, check in, sexual agreement?

What could I have done differently?

My Work/Life/Self-Care

Hours worked:

Did I get 7 hrs of sleep?

Did I play games or just sit in my chair for at least 15 minutes?

Did I get a full nonworking lunch?

Did I get two full days off from both offices in the last seven days?

Did I get 2 Matt evenings in the last seven days?

Did I work the number of hours that would keep me @/under 42hrs work, 18hrs/school?

Did I do recovery bookwork?

Did I do a WA meeting in the last seven days?

Did I make a recovery phone call or text?

What could I have done differently in any of the categories (reflection practice)?

PARTNER CONNECT Share what you learned about your work/life balance with your partner. Share the areas you identified as needing improvement.

The Hot Seat — Exercise 49

Note: This is a protocol we use in My Becoming Well Workgroups

Being In The Hot Seat
- The purpose of the hot seat is for you to get feedback on something that your relationship is struggling with.
- This is not to tear you down but build you up
- Guys need to have two topics ready: On SA or IA recovery
- If a guy doesn't come prepared, the 20 minutes is still given to that participant to dig into how the relationship is going and get feedback.
- Time Frame: 3 min. share, 15 min. feedback, & 2 min. action plan
- Victim Mindset is avoided

Giving Feedback
- Take Notes, Be Engaged, listen
- Think of a question that will dig deeper and uncover what's holding them back
- Target questions/sharpening for what actions they can take
- ALL feedback given is gentle with praises and sharpening purpose.
- NO feedback is to make the topic about you. ALL other members in the group are to ask questions for more details, praise/encourage them for sharing, OR give them a sharpening suggestion.
- Free Form - Any member in the group can jump in and start giving feedback during the 13-minute feedback loop.

Outcomes
- The guy in the Hot Seat states and personally records Action Items and/or Takeaways.
- Guys should be coming away from this with action items.
- The group is responsible for following up with the guy in the hot seat to keep them accountable to their action items. Phone calls are made to keep accountability at its highest.
- Guys are meant to leave the Hot Seat feeling empowered relationally.

Name two topics related to either your sexual addiction OR intimacy avoidance that you would want feedback on and bring to The Hot Seat. Why would did you choose these topics?

1. 2.	Why?

THE FOUNDATIONS OF RECOVERY - PART 2 DIGGING DEEPER

ALL Step Connection: One of the core purposes of the step process is to help build a community that relies upon one another, builds each other up, and holds one another accountable.

Describe how one of the steps relates to The Hot Seat.

PARTNER CONNECT Using your best self-reflection skills, share at least one thing you learned about yourself during the Hot Seat with your partner.

Recovery Travel Plan

Exercise 50

Written by Jeff H. from Oregon

Oftentimes when we travel, vacation, or get out of our normal routine, we can have problems. It's important to have a plan when we break our routine. Without a plan, we can flounder and white-knuckle our way through our trip. We may not be able to do recovery the same exact way as when we are home, but with a good plan we can stay close to our higher power and have a successful trip. Below is a worksheet to think through our trip, make decisions, and come up with a good plan. This only works if we implement our plan and put it into action when we are out.

Morning Prayer – The plan for my morning prayer is _____

Daily Reading – The plan for my daily reading is _____

Meetings – I will or will not be attending meetings during the trip? _____

Phone Calls – I will or will not be making calls during the trip? _____

Other Support – What are other ways I can have fellowship or get support during my travels? ___
_____

What are potential triggers I am anticipating during my travels? _____
_____

What is my plan to handle the triggers? _____
_____

Accountability – Who will I be accountable to during my trip? (This is at least one person I will keep in the loop as to how I am doing) _____

Other limitations – Are there other things I should limit or decide to withhold while I am on my trip? (Stuff like alcohol, watching TV alone, etc.) _____

_____

What is my emergency action plan in case I get off track? What adjustments will I make if I have more than one bad day and can't get back on track? _____

_____

Use the next page for examples to help complete your travel and vacation plan

MARATHON OF RECOVERY

Practices to maintain

- Daily check-in with my wife
- Reading of recovery materials
- Prayer (morning and evening)
- Making one call
- Exercise and time alone each day
- Attending regular group check-in (if occurring on that night and not flying)
- Keeping weekly accountability meeting (if occurring on that night and not flying)
- Adhering to 24-hour tell policy if applicable
- Rubber bands for wrist and around remote or any other possible boundary-violating object or place in the hotel room (as a reminder)
- Completing at least 1 page of at least 1 workbook/activity guide a day

Adhering to good sleep (all media off by 8 pm)

Consequences

If any of the above boundaries are violated, an accountability brother and partner must know within 24 hours and new consequences must be applied (written in stages, so that each consequence corresponds with a violation):

1. Twitter profile deleted
2. In-house separation
3. Out of house for 24 hours
4. Turning in smart phone for a pinwheel phone

Boundaries

- No staring at other women on the beach
- Before and after beach calls:
    - Sunday:
    - Monday:
    - Tuesday:
    - Wednesday:
- Side hugs only (on meeting and departure or when appropriate)
- No sexual contact of any kind
- No drinking/dancing/flirting with a woman
- No visits to any hotel room other than my own unless with another person
- No inordinate focus on chivalry (opening doors, paying for meals or physical/trait affirmations. This also includes grooming behaviors such as extensive use of pet names or excessive praise in forms such as putting hearts on text responses or excessively flowery words verbally/sexually)
- No prolonged (deep, embracing and longer than two seconds) chest-to-chest hugs with any women (Unless caught off guard or unavoidable, no chest-to-chest hugs at all).

PARTNER CONNECT Share your recovery travel and vacation plan with your partner.

Life in Recovery   Exercise 51

Many things can change going forward after this exercise book. Many things can stay the same. You will face decisions to either drift away from your partner, away from sexual addiction sobriety, and/or toward a healthy mindset and relationship with your higher power. It's your choice.

Below you will explore the ways you can choose to stay in recovery and a right relationship with your higher power.

Area of Recovery	How will you stay in Recovery?
Career	
Marriage Status	
Friendships	
Relationships with your Children	
Physical Health & Status of Sexual Diseases	
Feelings about Self	
Feelings about Others	
Spiritual Health	
Hobbies/Interests	
Other:	
Other:	

THE FOUNDATIONS OF RECOVERY - PART 2 DIGGING DEEPER

ALL Step Connection: Calling others in recovery and staying convicted and vulnerable about your actions and daily behaviors has been essential for your recovery. Make a call and share what you have planned for with your **most trusted recovery partner**. This can be your sponsor or someone you have bonded with throughout your time in recovery. Record any meaningful suggestions they had for staying in recovery.

Area of Recovery	How **they** said you stay in Recovery

Sponsoring Others

Exercise 52

Written by Jeff A. from Washington

You are on a path of recovery that has changed your heart. Your life before entering recovery has given you a story that is worth sharing and using to help others in their journey. Helping others will strengthen your recovery as well. Each time you share your story and encourage another person in theirs, you grow.

It is extraordinary to be an individual walking in recovery from sexual addiction or intimacy avoidance. You begin seeing the world differently and you can share this knowledge through sponsoring others that are not as far along as you.

Because you are at the end of this exercise book (approximately 1 year later), your first time through the 12-step process should be nearing its end. You have a story to tell through those steps. You have knowledge of what it takes to dig deep into inventory, confess your struggles to others, accept forgiveness for your wrongs, and make amends with those you've harmed. Now, you are attempting to live a life being honest, vulnerable, and reflective in a lifestyle that expresses your changed heart.

Choosing to sponsor someone is an honor. Consider someone in your recovery circle who is not as far along as you, someone who needs a sponsor. Approach them and ask if they would like a sponsor. Refer them to the "Choosing a Sponsor" exercise earlier in this book. If you both are open to walking in recovery together, commit to it. Set up typical times to talk. Know their sobriety date. Know their story. Use the space below to reflect on and set up commitments.

I chose to sponsor _____ and they agreed to have me.

We will typically connect _____ times per week on _____ (day(s) of week) at _____ (time).

Here is my story I would like to share…

_____
_____
_____
_____
_____
_____
_____
_____
_____
_____

I reflected and heard patterns and struggles in their story…

_____
_____
_____
_____
_____
_____
_____
_____
_____
_____
_____
_____
_____

Step 12 Connection: Write a prayer for them, speaking specifically on their areas of struggle, the partnership that needs healing, and for direction on how to approach being their sponsor.

Parting Words

In closing, I would like to thank you for using this workbook. We hope that it was helpful to you. While I know the road is long and tough to navigate, I encourage you to keep pressing on. As Winston Churchill once said, "If you are going through hell, keep going." If you do the work, don't give in, and seek help along the way, I know you will find your way out of the painful circumstances in which you have found yourself. We wish you healing, comfort, peace, and wholeness in your recovery journey.

Addendum

Yearly Tracker

Use this tracker combined with the weekly check-in to keep track of your efforts in recovery for the next year

Month	Dr/ N/R	Present in Relationship	Rating of Relationship	# of Calls	Recovery Score /100	Month	Dr/ N/R	Present in Relationship	Rating of Relationship	# of Calls	Recovery Score /100
Jan	/ /	/ 10	/ 10		/ 100	July	/ /	/ 10	/ 10		/ 100
	/ /	/ 10	/ 10		/ 100		/ /	/ 10	/ 10		/ 100
	/ /	/ 10	/ 10		/ 100		/ /	/ 10	/ 10		/ 100
	/ /	/ 10	/ 10		/ 100		/ /	/ 10	/ 10		/ 100
	/ /	/ 10	/ 10		/ 100		/ /	/ 10	/ 10		/ 100
Feb	/ /	/ 10	/ 10		/ 100	Aug	/ /	/ 10	/ 10		/ 100
	/ /	/ 10	/ 10		/ 100		/ /	/ 10	/ 10		/ 100
	/ /	/ 10	/ 10		/ 100		/ /	/ 10	/ 10		/ 100
	/ /	/ 10	/ 10		/ 100		/ /	/ 10	/ 10		/ 100
	/ /	/ 10	/ 10		/ 100		/ /	/ 10	/ 10		/ 100
March	/ /	/ 10	/ 10		/ 100	Sept	/ /	/ 10	/ 10		/ 100
	/ /	/ 10	/ 10		/ 100		/ /	/ 10	/ 10		/ 100
	/ /	/ 10	/ 10		/ 100		/ /	/ 10	/ 10		/ 100
	/ /	/ 10	/ 10		/ 100		/ /	/ 10	/ 10		/ 100
	/ /	/ 10	/ 10		/ 100		/ /	/ 10	/ 10		/ 100
April	/ /	/ 10	/ 10		/ 100	Oct	/ /	/ 10	/ 10		/ 100
	/ /	/ 10	/ 10		/ 100		/ /	/ 10	/ 10		/ 100
	/ /	/ 10	/ 10		/ 100		/ /	/ 10	/ 10		/ 100
	/ /	/ 10	/ 10		/ 100		/ /	/ 10	/ 10		/ 100
	/ /	/ 10	/ 10		/ 100		/ /	/ 10	/ 10		/ 100
May	/ /	/ 10	/ 10		/ 100	Nov	/ /	/ 10	/ 10		/ 100
	/ /	/ 10	/ 10		/ 100		/ /	/ 10	/ 10		/ 100
	/ /	/ 10	/ 10		/ 100		/ /	/ 10	/ 10		/ 100
	/ /	/ 10	/ 10		/ 100		/ /	/ 10	/ 10		/ 100
	/ /	/ 10	/ 10		/ 100		/ /	/ 10	/ 10		/ 100
June	/ /	/ 10	/ 10		/ 100	Dec	/ /	/ 10	/ 10		/ 100
	/ /	/ 10	/ 10		/ 100		/ /	/ 10	/ 10		/ 100
	/ /	/ 10	/ 10		/ 100		/ /	/ 10	/ 10		/ 100
	/ /	/ 10	/ 10		/ 100		/ /	/ 10	/ 10		/ 100
	/ /	/ 10	/ 10		/ 100		/ /	/ 10	/ 10		/ 100

Feeling Wheel

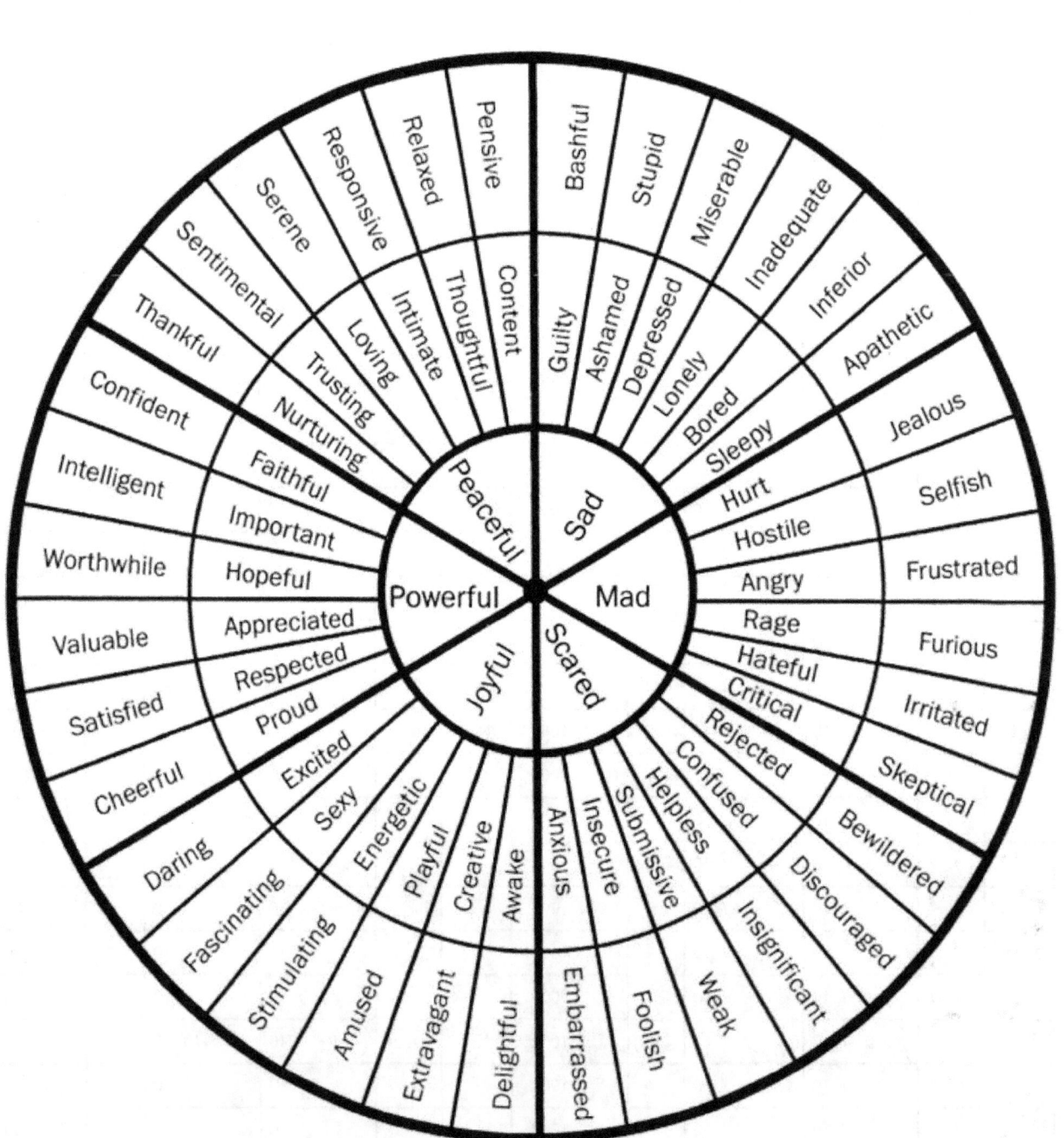

The Twelve Steps for Sexual Addiction

 **1** We admitted we were powerless over lust and that our lives had become unmanageable

 **2** We came to believe that a power greater than ourselves could restore us to sanity.

 **3** We made a decision to turn our will and lives over to the care of our higher power as we understand them.

 **4** We made a searching and fearless moral inventory of ourselves.

 **5** We admitted to our higher power, to ourselves, and to others the exact nature of our wrongs.

 **6** We were entirely ready to have our higher power remove all these defects of character.

 **7** We humbly asked our higher power to remove our struggle.

 **8** We made a list of all people we had harmed, and we became willing to make amends with them all.

 **9** We made direct amends to whomever possible, except when to do so would injure them or others.

 **10** We continue to take personal inventory and, when in the wrong, we promptly admit it.

 **11** We seek through prayer and meditation to improve contact with our higher power, praying for knowledge of their will for our lives and the strength to carry it out.

 **12** Having had a spiritual awakening from our experience through the steps, we seek to share with others and practice our principles in all our relationships.

The Twelve Steps for Intimacy Avoidance

 **1** We admitted we were powerless over avoidance and that our lives had become unmanageable

 **2** We came to believe that a power greater than ourselves could restore us to sanity.

 **3** We made a decision to turn our will and lives over to the care of our higher power as we understand them.

 **4** We made a searching and fearless moral inventory of ourselves.

 **5** We admitted to our higher power, to ourselves, and to others the exact nature of our wrongs.

 **6** We were entirely ready to have our higher power remove all these defects of character.

 **7** We humbly asked our higher power to remove our struggle.

 **8** We made a list of all people we had harmed, and we became willing to make amends with them all.

 **9** We made direct amends to whomever possible, except when to do so would injure them or others.

 **10** We continue to take personal inventory and, when in the wrong, we promptly admit it.

 **11** We seek through prayer and meditation to improve contact with our higher power, praying for knowledge of their will for our lives and the strength to carry it out.

 **12** Having had a spiritual awakening from our experience through the steps, we seek to share with others and practice our principles in all our relationships.

Recovery and 12 Step Prayers

Third Step Prayer (Page 63, AA Big Book)

God, I offer myself to Thee — to build with me and to do with me as Thou wilt. Relieve me of the bondage of self, that I may better do Thy will. Take away my difficulties, that victory over them may bear witness to those I would help of Thy Power, Thy Love, and Thy Way of life. May I do Thy will always!

Fourth Step Prayer (Page 67, AA Big Book)

This is a sick man. How can I be helpful to him? God, save me from being angry. Thy will be done.

Seventh Step Prayer (Page 76, AA Big Book)

My Creator, I am now willing that you should have all of me, good & bad. I pray that you now remove from me every single defect of character that stands in the way of my usefulness to you & my fellows. Grant me strength, as I go from here to do Your bidding. Amen.

Eighth Step Prayer (Page 76, AA Big Book)

Faith without works is dead.

Tenth Step Prayer (Page 85, AA Big Book)

How can I serve Thee? Thy will (not mine) be done.

Eleventh Step Prayer (Twelve Steps and Twelve Traditions, p. 99)

Lord, make me a channel of Thy peace – that where there is hatred, I may bring love – that where there is wrong, I may bring the spirit of forgiveness – that where there is discord, I may bring harmony – that where there is error, I may bring truth--that where there is doubt, I may bring faith--that where there is despair, I may bring hope – that where there are shadows, I may bring light – that where there is sadness, I may bring joy. Lord, grant that I may seek to comfort rather than to be comforted – to understand, than to be understood – to love, than to be loved. For it is by self-forgetting that one finds. It is by forgiving that one is forgiven. It is by dying that one awakens to eternal life. Amen

Serenity Prayer (Reinhold Niebuhr)

God, grant me the serenity to accept the things I cannot change,
The courage to change the things I can,
And the wisdom to know the difference.

40 ways to be IA
(Intimacy Avoidant)

1. **Marked lack of empathy.** Has trouble putting themselves in someone else's shoes. Often comes off as insensitive or uncaring. When others try to share their perspective, they often impose their own views on the situation without listening to the other person's view. Often has trouble understanding cause and effect - in other words, how their actions are contributing to the reactions of others.

2. **Oversensitivity to criticism or perceives criticism when there is none.** This may stem from a fear of rejection, poor self-esteem, or a generally negative view of others' intentions. Oversensitivity to criticism has been linked to negative childhood experiences such as harsh criticism from a parent or caregiver, rejection from peers, or having a parent with unrealistically high expectations. People who are oversensitive to criticism (real or perceived) often have negative cognitive biases that cause them to interpret information in a negative way.

3. **Low emotional expression and bandwidth.** Has an inability or unwillingness (oftentimes both) to express emotion. Emotional range is generally very small (2 or 3 emotions shared, usually some type of anger). The term "emotional bandwidth" refers to someone's ability to handle or engage in emotional stimuli, whether the stimulus is their own or someone else's.

4. **Jumps to conclusions.** Involves jumping to conclusions without having supporting facts. Mind-reading is when people randomly conclude that others are reacting negatively to them. Fortune-telling is assuming things are going to turn out badly and acting like those assumptions are already established facts.

5. **Contempt for self/others.** Contempt for self often comes across as shame and/or self-pity. Contempt for others comes out as grandiosity, belittling, or criticism.

6. **Sabotages emotional connectedness.** According to research studies, people who sabotage their relationships often have low self-esteem, difficulty trusting people (especially their partners), and a fear of commitment or being hurt, abandoned, or rejected.

7. **Reactive vs. Proactive in relationships.** This person appears ambivalent or disinterested in creating opportunities for ongoing, consistent connectedness. Major efforts to show love to their partner only come when the partner is fed up and entertaining the thought of ending the relationship. These efforts often fade away once the partner is reconnected to them, leading to an ongoing cycle that alternates between disinterest, emotional pain, and love-bombing.

8. **Spiritually independent or disengaged.** This person refuses to share any intimate details of their spirituality with their partner, often claiming that their spirituality is "private".

9. **Hoop jumping.** Often a feature of Intimacy Avoidant relationships, the IA will make their partner jump through a series of "hoops" to receive love. Much of this behavior is born out of entitlement. IAs often use this behavior as an excuse to withhold intimacy from their partner or criticize them for a "lack of performance."

10. **Defensiveness.** Defensive people often have issues of power and control. They often perceive confrontation and/or accountability as threats. The purpose of defensiveness is typically to protect a person from feeling hurt or shame. Defensiveness comes in many forms, including blame-shifting, silence, denial, and even self-pity.

11. **Prideful and/or Unteachable.** Typically, a person is masking feelings of low self-esteem and self-worth with pride. Pride is often a byproduct of feelings of inadequacy and vulnerability. Being "unteachable" can stem from pride, jealousy, stress, anxiety, or feelings of inadequacy.

12. **Blame-shifting.** People who blame-shift are often in denial about their level of personal responsibility. They often can't accept the fact that they may be at least partially responsible for a failure or mistake. Another reason for blame-shifting is to make the other person feel guilty or shamed, to silence them.

13. **Offended from victim position.** This takes place when a person decides that their role as victim gives them the right to lash out and/or hurt others. Pia Mellody and Terrence Real call this "retaliation." Intimacy Avoidant people often put themselves in the victim position through blame-shifting, shame, and self-pity. This makes it easier to justify bad behavior.

14. **Suspicious of partner.** There are many reasons IAs are suspicious of their partners. Common reasons include adverse childhood experiences that cause a general lack of trust toward others, depression and anxiety, and negative experiences in past relationships.

15. **Gaslighting.** Gaslighting is defined as psychological manipulation, typically over a prolonged period, that causes the victim to question their thoughts, feelings, memories, and perception of reality. Gaslighting typically involves lying but is not the same as lying. People often lie to escape consequences. Gaslighters lie to intentionally cause someone else to doubt themselves.

16. **Stonewalling/Punishing through anger.** Uses anger or silence to control the conversation. With silence, the partner eventually gives up, which is the intent. Anger is often used to intimidate, and punishing through anger is done purposely to teach the person a lesson and make them think twice about saying anything again. In either case, both are being used to silence someone.

17. **Frequent lying.** For IAs, lying often comes in the form of leaving out important information to avoid unwanted consequences. In some cases, habitual lying can be a sign of a more serious personality disorder.

18. **Avoids taking responsibility for actions.** This can be a result of emotional immaturity, denial, a refusal to be vulnerable, or an avoidance of intense feelings of remorse, guilt, and/or shame. In more serious cases, it can be because the person truly feels that accepting consequences is beneath them or does not have any understanding that their actions have consequences.

19. **Breadcrumbing or Love Bombing.** Breadcrumbing is a form of manipulation in which a person gives another person just enough attention and/or love to string them along. Love bombing often comes in the form of excessive flattery, attention, or gifts being used to lure someone to gain security for themselves.

20. **Emotionally disengaged.** This often stems from a deep fear of being ridiculed or rejected. An emotionally disengaged person may have learned from previous relationships that showing emotions made them vulnerable to negative consequences. Emotional disengagement is often developed in the family of origin when one or both parents failed to communicate their emotions or were uncomfortable with the emotions of others.

21. **Feelings are facts.** A person who treats feelings as facts often experiences emotions so intensely that they feel real. This typically stems from emotional immaturity. It's related to the cognitive distortion of emotional reasoning: "I feel it, so it must be true."

22. **Poor self-reflection.** Otherwise known as a lack of self-awareness. People with poor self-reflection are often intensely afraid of judgement and rejection from others. They keep themselves in a "protective bubble." This "bubble" makes it difficult for them to get in touch with their inner selves.

23. **Self-preoccupation.** This often stems from early childhood experiences of feeling rejected by others. They also could have been brought up to believe that they didn't have to consider the feelings of others. Trauma can also play a role because the person may have learned that they couldn't trust others, and this developed into self-preoccupation. Self-preoccupied people are generally emotionally immature.

24. **Labels themselves and others.** Related to the cognitive distortion of Labeling, which is a form of overgeneralization. It can also be related to perfectionism. For example, instead of being able to accept that they made a mistake, a person might label themselves a "loser." Instead of being understanding about the faults of others, they may label others "losers" or "idiots." Instead

of describing a situation realistically, labeling typically involves using inflammatory terms and language.

25. **Focuses on the faults of others.** Typically used as a defense mechanism in order to avoid feelings of guilt, shame, or inadequacy. It can also stem from entitlement when a person feels everyone else it at fault for them not getting what they want or feel they deserve.

26. **Objectification.** Treats their partner, others, and even themselves as objects. This extends far past sexual objectification or reducing someone to the sum of their body parts. Objectification also shows up as treating someone as if there is no need to be concerned about their experiences and/or feelings, a refusal to honor boundaries, treating people as if they were tools to be used for the IA to achieve their own goals, and treating someone as if they were easily replaced with someone else (a refusal to acknowledge someone's uniqueness).

27. **Poor demeanor.** Acts frequently disgruntled, angry, or irritated. Doesn't listen to their partner's feelings or discounts their experience. When asked to participate in the nurturing of the relationship, acts like it's a huge imposition. When asked to be accountable for past and/or present actions, responds with anger, blame, or pouting.

28. **Sexually disconnected or avoidant.** Doesn't make eye contact during sex or is mentally "checked out." Sex often feels empty and transactional to the partner. Also common is a complete/almost complete avoidance of sex. Couples that have sex 6 or fewer times per year are considered to have a "sexless" relationship.

29. **Sexual gratification outside of committed relationship.** This isn't always the case, but when it is it's typically due to an inability to connect with the partner. For most, this will be done through pornography and masturbation. For some, it will involve getting emotionally or sexually connected with a real person who is not their partner. Sexual addiction and attachment disorders are often underlying issues, especially with serial cheating.

30. **Inability to handle conflict productively.** For some, this will show up as conflict avoidance, stonewalling, and/or people-pleasing. For others, this will involve blame-shifting, denial, and overall defensiveness.

31. **All-or-nothing thinking (black-and-white thinking).** Seeing things in black and white without shades of gray. Tends to associate others and self into 2 categories: good and bad. Signs of all-or-nothing thinking include a tendency to use extreme terms when describing things, perfectionism, inability to see both good and bad in people and/or self, negative self-talk, and fear of trying new things.

32. **An intense need to be right.** Possible reasons for always needing to be right include insecurity, a need for control, a fear of failure, a competitive nature, and cognitive biases or distortions (such as all-or-nothing thinking) that make it difficult to consider alternate perspectives or admit it when wrong.

33. **Easily offended.** Often related to the cognitive distortion of personalization, which is assigning blame to oneself for circumstances out of one's control. Other reasons include unresolved psychological or emotional issues, a perception that their honor or personally held beliefs are being attacked, a generally negative emotional state, or the struggle to consider another's point of view.

34. **Maximization and minimization of faults and/or good deeds.** Tends to see others' faults as "huge" and their own as "not so bad." Tends to see their contributions as "huge" and others' contributions as minimal. In extreme cases, this can be due to grandiosity that contributes to a false sense of self-importance.

35. **Workaholism.** Many workaholics seek approval and become overly focused on work and "busyness" to gain approval and respect from others. Sometimes workaholism also occurs when the person is trying to avoid intimacy in their relationships.

36. **Plays the victim.** Playing the victim is a manipulative tactic. It is often used to avoid taking responsibility, gain sympathy and attention from others, and/or to discredit the experience and feelings of a person they have wronged.

37. **Hero or Zero.** Since IAs tend to see things in black and white without shades of gray, they tend to see themselves as a complete "hero" without faults or a "zero" with nothing but faults. This mentality often leads to blame-shifting, going "victim," and even complete denial of the issues.

38. **I did it my way.** This is an unwillingness to accept influence from their partner. IAs are typically highly independent and often don't listen to the suggestions of their partners when making decisions. Many partners define an IA partner as "an island."

39. **Cynical Script.** A bad story being played repeatedly in the person's head to excuse their poor treatment of the partner. The cynical script is often used to play the victim.

40. **Married but Unloved:** If married, the partner feels as if they are alone in it all. Many partners married to Intimacy Avoidants describe this as a surprise. It is common for Intimacy Avoidants to act differently before marriage than after marriage. Once the commitment to marriage is made, Intimacy Avoidants start to pull away from their partners in the ways that matter most. Partners may describe the relationship as sexless, devoid of intimacy, and disconnected.

Workgroups and Intensives

Men's Becoming Well Workgroups

Some guys have been in groups before; others have not. If you're committed to recovery from Sexual Addiction, Intimacy Avoidance, or Infidelity and are committed to rebuilding trust in your marriage, then our Men's Becoming Well Workgroups will be a good fit for you. Our men's groups focus on building and maintaining integrity, restoring intimacy in relationships, and rebuilding trust. They concentrate on two things: how to stop acting out and be accountable for the behavior that is breaking trust in the relationship, and how to develop the character and empathy it will take to support the relationship moving forward. And unlike many recovery groups out there, our guys are both finding sobriety and maintaining it.

Our groups are led by trained facilitators who have walked through many of these issues themselves, know how to stay sober, and know how to win in their relationship. The groups are small in size (no more than 8 people) so that each person can get the attention they need to address specific issues.

Each week, participants will hear a teaching from a trained professional and receive assignments and exercises that facilitate recovery for both themselves and their relationships. Participants will also have access to an online education portal, videos that explain the concepts talked about during group, and tutorials on how to work exercises and complete assignments.

Another thing that makes our groups different is that we welcome input from the wounded partners. Most programs exclude the partner, expecting that they stay in a relationship and take their partner's word for it that they're doing the work. When we hear from partners about past experiences, they often complain that nothing was shared with them, and they didn't even know what was going on most of the time.

Although we want to stress that the men need to own and work through their own recovery, and no partner can do that for them, we assign exercises to include the partner in rebuilding the relationship. Additionally, we offer a free monthly video conference call in which we update partners on what the guys will be working on that month and allow them to ask questions. Those meetings are typically led by Matt and Laura Burton personally.

Join a Men's Becoming Well workgroup today
www.BecomingWellInstitute.com

Men's Sexual Addiction, Infidelity & Intimacy Avoidance Recovery Intensives

Sexual addiction, infidelity, and intimacy avoidance can be isolating. Whether they're recovering from physical or emotional affairs, infidelity through pornography or other forms of sexual acting out, or intimacy avoidance, men entering recovery often feel like they are going it alone. Maximize your intensive experience by joining with other men to work through issues common to sexual addiction, infidelity, and intimacy avoidance. A Men's 3-Day Recovery Intensive can provide you with a safe environment to voice your pain and concerns, and to learn techniques for healing.

Intensives in a group format provide hope that you are not alone. You will hear the stories and struggles of others. You will also hear from Laura Burton, a trained and certified coach and a partner of someone who struggled with intimacy avoidance and pornography addiction. This will allow you to gain a deeper understanding of what both you and your partner are experiencing during this tough time in your relationship. You will not only see things through your relationship's historical lens, but through the eyes of others. This can help you gain a much-needed perspective that will help you move forward in recovery. Intensives focus on breaking the hold that addiction, infidelity, and intimacy avoidance have had on you and your partner. We partner with you to solve the issues that are holding you back from having the connection you have always wanted.

The Men's 3-Day Recovery Intensive offers daily group meetings and instruction by experts to ensure that the experience is tailored to you. Contact us today to schedule your intensive. Even if you are not currently in a relationship, the perspective you will gain throughout the intensive will help prepare you for the future—however that may look.

- Intensives are limited to 14 men per session.
- They take place at the Becoming Well Institute Intensive Center in sunny Tucson, Arizona.
- This includes an intake and assessment to identify your specific needs.
- We currently offer 2 distinct intensives for men: one with a focus on intimacy avoidance and one with a focus on sexual addiction and sexual/emotional infidelity.
- Each intensive is comprised of a combination of workgroups, group education, homework, exercises to work on with your partner, and personalized recovery plans.
- Contact us for pricing.

Our intensive center is located in beautiful, sunny Tucson, Arizona.

Learn more or sign up for a Men's Recovery Intensive today
www.BecomingWellInstitute.com

Sober Is Not Well
Men's "Going Deeper" Healing Intensives

Are you working on your recovery from porn/sexual addiction and intimacy avoidance? If so, why is your marriage still struggling so much and why do you still have behaviors and/or belief systems that are stunting you and your marriage from truly becoming well?

Why are you still stuck? Why aren't you getting a lot better? Why isn't your marriage getting a lot better? Because Sober is not Well. The areas underlying the SA and IA must be addressed. It's time to take another step in your recovery journey and focus on the roots.

In the Men's "Going Deeper" Healing Intensive, you'll focus on 4 specific areas of the 16 roots that slow or block recovery. These areas will be identified through a 2-part assessment process, one with you and the other getting your partner's input. You will spend your intensive time focused on the 4 identified focus areas in a process we call "Depth Work." That work will happen throughout the 3 ½-day intensive. The 16 root areas of potential intensive focus are:

Past Hurts Focus: Healing the injuries of your past to lessen their impact on you today and in the future.

o Trauma Focus; o Loss Focus; o Neglect Focus; o Abandonment Focus

Adaptive Behaviors Focus: Dismantling recurring struggles that are destroying you and/or your marriage and have you stuck.

o Other Addictions/Addiction Swapping Focus; o Anger Focus; o Specific Avoidance Focus; o Sexless Marriage Focus (Relational Sexual Avoidance); o Shame Focus; o Chronic Lying Focus; o Low or Lack of Empathy Focus; o Over Controlling of Self & Others' Focus; o Narcissistic Characteristics Focus; o Perpetual Victim Focus; o Emotional Immaturity Focus; o Chronic Negative Thinking Focus

The Details:

- Men's Healing Intensives are limited to 14 men per week.
- Healing Intensives take place on Thursday-Sunday.
- Your intensive will include intake assessment sessions to identify your particular needs.
- Each intensive weekend is comprised of groups, learning, processing, specific exercises, and personalized recovery plans.
- The time commitment per day is approximately 8 hours.
- Healing Intensive weekends are offered in-person only.

Our intensive center is located in beautiful, sunny Tucson, Arizona.

www.BecomingWellInstitute.com

Couple's Group Intensives
Moving couples from "Shattered to Strong"

Sexual addiction, infidelity, and intimacy avoidance can be isolating. Couples entering recovery often feel like they are going through it alone. Maximize your intensive experience by joining with other couples to work through issues common to infidelity and intimacy avoidance. A Couple's Group Intensive can provide you with a safe environment to voice your pain, concerns, and learn techniques for healing. Often, couples working through infidelity feel alone, judged, and hopeless. Intensives in a group format provide hope that you are not alone. You will hear the stories and struggles of others. This will allow you to gain a deeper understanding of what you and your partner are going through during this crisis. You will not only see things through your relationship's historical lens but also through the eyes of others. This can help you gain a much-needed perspective that will move you forward in recovery.

Group Intensive Weekends offer daily group meetings, instruction by experts, and individual sessions to help ensure that your experience is tailor-made for you. Couples leave feeling validated, understood, and hopeful— even if they were initially nervous about sharing their experience with others. Group Intensive Weekends will allow you to make connections with other people who understand what you are going through. This makes it possible for you to receive ongoing support through the relationships you form over the weekend. Couples will leave the Intensive with three distinct recovery plans: one for the wounding partner, one for the wounded partner, and one for the relationship.

- For couples who are in crisis after the recent discovery or disclosure of infidelity.
- For couples who are stuck and don't know how to get better.
- For couples who have experienced the isolation of infidelity, addiction, and intimacy avoidance and want to join a community of people who understand.
- For couples who want to learn from the experience of others in a safe environment.
- For couples who have done recovery work and want to deepen their experience.
- For couples who need a safe space to deal with what happened without feeling judged.
- For couples who want to hear from experts on how to recover from infidelity.
- For couples who want to accomplish in 3 days what normally takes 4-6 months.

The Details:

- Group Intensives take place in person on Thursday, Friday, and Saturday.
- Group Intensive Weekends include intake and assessment sessions to identify your specific needs.
- Each Group Intensive Weekend is comprised of a combination of workgroups, learning, homework, couple-specific exercises, and personalized recovery plans.
- The time commitment per day for Intensive Weekends is approximately 8-10 hours.

Learn more or sign up for a Couple's Group Intensive today
www.BecomingWellInstitute.com

Couples 7-Day: All In One Group Intensives

Are you a guy or married to a guy who's stuck or in a downward spiral, relationally or in your individual recovery, and who's unable to do what's needed/necessary to heal the shattered trust in your relationship?

What if you could experience all 4 intensives that Becoming Well Institute offers in a week? This means he could get the help he needs for his addiction and/or avoidance, as well as begin to heal the roots that created them. At the same time, she could begin to heal from a broken heart and shattered trust. You, as a couple, could begin to repair what has to date seemed impossible to heal.

Well, you can do all this through our 7-day All-In-One Intensive. At this intensive, the woman does key segments of the Women's Wounded Partner Intensive with other women also attending. The man does key segments of the Men's Recovery Intensive and Men's Going Even Deeper Intensive with the other men. Both partners work through key segments of the Couples Group intensive together, with the focus on helping couples navigate SA and IA recovery and Rebuilding Trust.

The four intensives that this all-in-one draws from:

- The Men's Recovery Intensive is for men striving to find lasting sobriety from porn addiction, sexual addiction, physical infidelity, emotional infidelity, intimacy avoidance, and/or sexual avoidance.
- The Wounded Partners Healing Intensive is for partners impacted by their wounding partner's sexual betrayal, intimacy avoidance, and/or sexual avoidance behaviors.
- The Men's "Going Deeper" Healing Intensives focus on the roots that created the addictive and destructive behaviors.
- The Couples Group Intensive helps couples understand what couple recovery looks like and what it takes to repair and rebuild the relationship, especially in the area of trust. It creates clarity and understanding of whether the wounding partner is serious about recovery and what the wounded partner should expect. It also creates a deeper understanding of what the benchmarks and timelines are for healing, all while supplying the tools and practice necessary to increase the likelihood for success.
- BONUS: Our All-In-One Intensive also teaches you how to help your School-Age and Adult Children Heal from the impacts of SA and IA.

For less than half of the total combined cost of all four intensives, you can experience them all. More importantly, you both benefit from the increased recovery & healing each intensive brings.

This is a great option for anyone wanting to accelerate the healing process, because intensives condense 4-6 months' worth of session work into 7 days.

Learn more or sign up for a Guys Group Intensive today
www.BecomingWellInstitute.com

Private Couple's Intensive
Moving couples from "Shattered to Strong"

Couples that attend Our One-on-One Private Couple's Intensives say it helps them understand and begin or advance the long journey of healing from the immediate and ongoing impacts of porn addiction, sexual addiction, infidelity &/or Intimacy avoidance - for both the Wounding and Wounded partner. We are able to take the time to deep-dive into what's specifically destroying the trust, individually and as a couple, and find the recovery you're desperately trying to either rediscover or discover for the first time.

For many couples, this intensive is their last stop before divorce court or a decision to stay permanent roommates. Couple after couple says that their time at the intensive allowed them to identify and begin the process of healing the hurt and devastation, as well as giving them a new relational system, as their current one just doesn't work for many reasons.

If you choose a Private Couple's Intensive, we will work with you to identify your specific needs to make sure your concerns are fully addressed in a private setting. Our Private Couple's Intensives are 3 days in length and will address both people in the relationship individually as well as the relationship itself.

Like the Guys Group Intensive, our Private Couple's Intensive is a great option for anyone wanting to accelerate the healing process, because intensives take 4-6 months' worth of session work and condense it into 3 days. You will receive an assessment of your unique issues, 7-8 hours per day of instruction, exercises and tools to help you move forward, and a personalized recovery plan for yourself and/or your relationship. We provide you a shame-free environment to address your specific issues.

And, if you choose a Private Couple's Intensive, we want you to know that partners are always treated with respect, compassion, and validation for the pain that their partner's issues have caused them. As a partner, you will never be blamed or asked to take any responsibility for your partner's choices. Also, if desired, we have full disclosure and polygraph services available.

Learn more or sign up for a Private Couple's Intensive today
www.BecomingWellInstitute.com

Books and Courses

Moving Couples from Shattered to Strong

REBUILDING TRUST

A Couple's Guide to Healing After Betrayal

MATT BURTON
LAURA BURTON

www.BecomingWellInstitute.com

Books and Courses

Moving Couples from Shattered to Strong

REBUILDING  TRUST

FOR CHRISTIANS

A Couple's Guide to Healing After Betrayal

**MATT BURTON
LAURA BURTON**

www.BecomingWellInstitute.com

Books and Courses

Moving Partners from Shattered to Strong

Mending After Betrayal

BOOK AND WORKBOOK

LAURA BURTON

www.BecomingWellInstitute.com

Books and Courses

Moving Partners from Shattered to Strong

Mending After Betrayal

BOOK AND WORKBOOK FOR CHRISTIANS

LAURA BURTON

www.BecomingWellInstitute.com

Books and Courses

www.BecomingWellInstitute.com

Books and Courses

www.BecomingWellInstitute.com

Books and Courses

www.BecomingWellInstitute.com

Books and Courses

Books and Courses

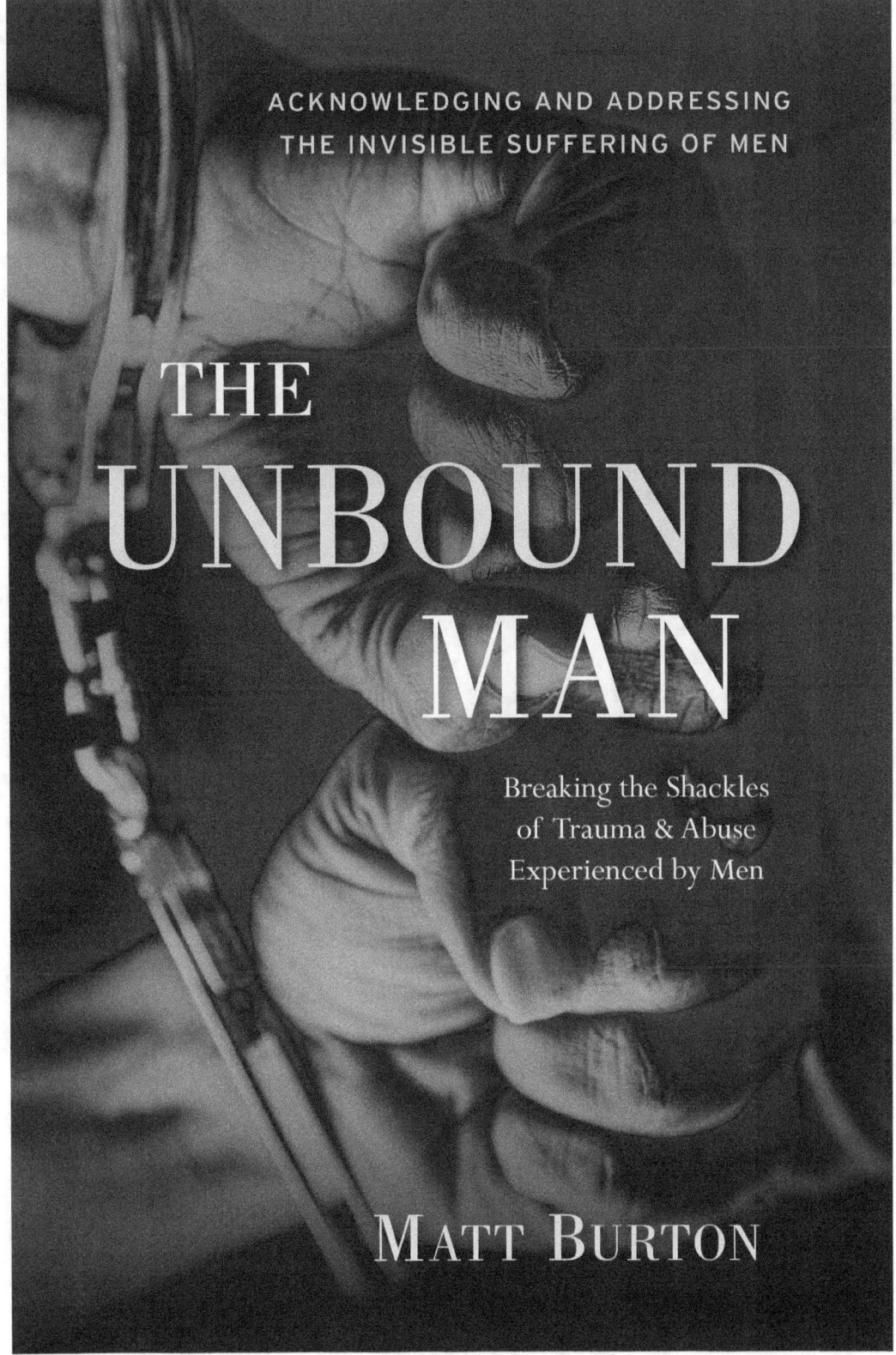

www.BecomingWellInstitute.com

Books and Courses

ACKNOWLEDGING AND ADDRESSING
THE INVISIBLE SUFFERING OF MEN

THE UNBOUND MAN

FOR CHRISTIANS

Breaking the Shackles
of Trauma & Abuse
Experienced by Men

Matt Burton

www.BecomingWellInstitute.com

Books and Courses

Books and Courses

Books and Courses

Books and Courses

Connect with Us

 www.facebook.com/mybecomingwell

 Becoming Well (@mybecomingwell)

 Becoming Well (@mybecomingwell)

 www.mybecomingwell.com

 info@mybecomingwell.com

 520-355-5322

www.ingramcontent.com/pod-product-compliance
Lightning Source LLC
LaVergne TN
LVHW081457060526
838201LV00057BA/3060